Twin Flame Obsession

(Book 1 in The Twin Flame Magnetism Series™)

Also by Dr. Harmony:

Twin Flame Code Breaker: 11 Key Codes
(English & Spanish Editions)

Twin Flame Ascension™: Take Me Home Oracle Deck

Twin Flame Confessions: Stories of Love, Loss & Lessons on the Journey to Union

Champ The Human Whisperer

www.TwinFlameExpert.com

www.AscensionAcademyOnline.com

www.OrganizedBookBlueprint.com

www. SoulWritersAcademy.com

www.StrutLikeYourMutt.com

www.GlobalPawsForPeace.org

This book is Book 1 of the Twin Flame Magnetism™ Series—a transformational series guiding you from obsession to wholeness, detachment to embodiment, and ultimately toward the kind of love that starts from within. Continue the journey with future books and resources designed to empower your path.

Twin Flame Obsession

(Book 1 in The Twin Flame Magnetism™ Series)

Break the Spell, Take Back Your Power & Become the Flame

Dr. Harmony

HARMONY Lighthouse
PUBLISHING

Sedona, Arizona

Twin Flame Obsession (Book 1 in The Twin Flame Magnetism Series™): *Break the Spell, Take Back Your Power & Become the Flame*

Published by *Harmony Lighthouse Publishing*

First Edition, 2025

ISBN: 979-8-9915090-3-9

Library of Congress Cataloging-in-Publication Data

Harmony, Dr.

Twin Flame Obsession (Book 1 in The Twin Flame Magnetism Series™): Break the Spell, Take Back Your Power & Become the Flame by Dr. Harmony — 1st ed.

Summary: This book is a raw and revealing guide that exposes the truth behind chasing love that doesn't chase you back. As the first book in *The Twin Flame Magnetism Series™*, it helps you break the spell of longing, reclaim your energy, and begin the journey back to yourself.

1. Relationships — Twin flame aspects. 2. Love — Religious aspects. 3. Self-realization — Spirituality.

Library of Congress Control Number (LCCN): 2025915720

Disclaimer: This book is intended for informational and educational purposes only. The content within this book does not constitute medical, psychological, or veterinary advice. Always seek the advice of your physician, mental health professional, or veterinarian with any questions you may have regarding a medical condition or mental health issues. Reliance on any information provided in this book is solely at your own risk.

Printed in the United States of America.

For more information about the author, upcoming books, and events, please visit www.TwinFlameExpert.com.

REFLECTIONS FROM THE FLAME

"There's a lot I could say about this beautiful offering from my dear friend Harmony…But mostly, I just want to breathe and say thank you. Mainly because this isn't just a book. It's a deeply channeled transmission of love that doesn't try to teach you anything (although the tools are FANTASTIC).

And reminds you of what you already are. As I read these early chapters, something unexpected started to happen. Old shadows began to stir. Heart beating loudly… Memories. The feelings I had already been experiencing during the week resurfaced once more. That alone told me how powerful this work is: not just in concept, but in energy.

I grew up as a little boy where love wore a mask wrapped in conditions, expectations, and unspoken rules. And even now, those old codes still unwind in my system.

Harmony's words didn't just speak to that part of me; they opened a door for something softer to come in & wrap itself around my darkness.

As a teen, I experienced abuse at the hands of an older man. It taught me to fear the masculine to disconnect from my own inner strength, my own "twin flame," my own steady presence.

But as I read, I could feel a new kind of safety landing in my body. A sense that wholeness was never something I had to find… just something I had to ALLOW out.

This book doesn't ask you to become anything.
It meets you where you are with a kiss and a cuddle.
Singing the only objective truth out there: You're already home."

— Harrison Meagher, *Author, Mentor, Channel*

"Dr. Harmony writes with a rare blend of simplicity and depth, reminding us of truths we've long forgotten but are slowly beginning to remember... remembering to walk through the darkness of pain and suffering to a new beginning. A way we've wanted but never felt safe or familiar. We tend to choose old patterns that were easy, despite our discomfort and the obvious red flags, convincing ourselves that this time would be different.

She guides us on the longest and hardest journey we will ever take: the 18 inches from our stinking thinking in our head to the beautiful place within our hearts. In this sacred space, we re-root ourselves and become the fruitful tree we were always meant to be.

This book is for you if you're searching for a lover, a flame, care, or safety—start by learning to love and care for yourself. Feel the warmth of your own flame. Love you first. Love you always. Love you only... Always."

— Anthony J Rodriguez *Walking Crow,*
Author of Transformation of a Walking Crow

"Chapter 5—*Trapped in the Trauma Loop*—did strike my soul. As an oncology nurse, I've walked through a lot of pain with others— but this chapter touched a very personal place in me. I am that woman who learned from infancy that love was uncertain, filled with chaos and contraction.

When I finally chose safe love, my family came after me. They tried to spoil the joy and peace I had finally found, shattering my hopes of having that sacred space. It was a lie.

But I'm so grateful that we have life lessons—and amazing wisdom from women like Dr. Harmony—who share truth and spur on the freedom, peace, and love we are all meant to know. The love of self and for the God who created us.

May you continue to be blessed, dear soul. Hugs from PA."

— Lisa Marie Basile, *RN*

"This book blew my mind and went straight to the core of my heart. It struck a chord in me that I had been burying or doing a side-step dance with for a while. The words echoed the emotions of my own heart, emotions I have long since silenced, even to myself. This has reinforced for me that my true path to wholeness has not been realized yet because I haven't allowed myself to fully embrace the pain of separation that I felt from letting go of the part of me that felt the most alive and the most in pain. I've simply put band-aids on a wound that has yet to heal.

Reading it felt like a soft balm to a deep ache in my heart and a void in my soul—the place that has yet to come home. It hit pain points I had been trying to rise above, all the while knowing the only way out was through the full expression of them.

It is filled with the wisdom and the heart to enable me to do just that. Harmony's words transported me back to a realm that has always defied time and space- where only unconditional love exists.

There are not many people on this earth who can capture the depth, the beauty, and the learnings from the pain quite like Harmony.

This book isn't just about twin flames or romantic love—it can apply to any kind of soul love, the one that can stay with you for eternity.

The message is for anyone who is looking to come home to themselves in a world where they have felt pain and love unlike anything else ever experienced."

— Sabrina Khalliya, *Integrative Energy Healer: Specializing in Vortex Healing, Biofeedback, and Flower Essence Therapy*

"Devoid of spiritual guidance, the human body-mind complex does what it has evolved to do: learn survival tactics and replay them when a future stimulus looks and feels similar to the original stimulus. Romantic and sexual relationships are often built off of the same survival programs that brought us satisfaction or survival in the past. Spiritual work in this context involves identifying triggers and choosing outcomes that are more aligned with love, joy, and peace.

Dr. Harmony leads the way in helping readers regain a sense of acceptance and balance within themselves, enabling them to show up with love and reciprocity in their relationships with others. Seen through the lens of trauma conditioning, relationships are the mirror reflecting what most needs addressing in ourselves. This starts with decoding the trauma/addiction response.

In this book she offers a birds-eye view of the levels of relationship that lead to mutually beneficial harmonious exchange. I appreciate the guidance in rising above my natural programming to what serves the highest good of my Self and my partner."

— Mark E Thompson, *MD,*
Anesthesiologist and Reiki Practitioner

To the ones who walked through the fire—
barefoot, broken, and still burning with hope.

To the ones who loved so deeply it shattered them—
and still had the courage to rise from the ashes.

To the ones who thought they lost themselves
but found their power in the wreckage.

This is for you.
For your ache, your awakening, your becoming.
For the flame you tried to chase—
only to realize… it was always you.

May these pages be the permission slip
to stop waiting, stop chasing, and finally choose you.

CONTENTS

Introduction

You may think you're holding a book—but what you're really holding is a match. A match that, once lit, won't just burn the illusion... it will ignite your truth.

So read carefully. Only if you're ready to burn the story down—and rise in your own name.

WARNING: This book will piss off your ego before it sets your soul free. If you're looking for a way to get them back, this isn't it. If you want another fluffy affirmation that they're your twin flame and "meant to return,"—you won't find that here either. But if you're sick of the endless spirals, the silent treatments, the psychic readings that keep contradicting each other, the sleepless nights, and the pain that won't let go... then keep reading. Because I wrote this for the version of you, that's breaking. For the person who's checked every sign, pulled every card, begged the Universe for one more dream just to hold on. I see you. I was you. And I know the hell you're living through.

This isn't a book about getting them back—it's about breaking the spell that made you forget your own power... and becoming the flame you thought they were.

Because obsession isn't love—it's a trauma response. It's the illusion that someone else holds the key to your healing, your happiness, and your wholeness. And that illusion is seductive. It's spiritual. It's wrapped in angel numbers, divine timing, and soul contracts. But underneath all of that? It's pain. It's powerlessness. It's the silent scream of a person who keeps abandoning themselves in the name of "unconditional love."

Twin Flame Obsession exposes the real cost of chasing a love that's not chasing you back. It unhooks you from the fantasy, shows you where the addiction lives in your body, and walks you back to your power. Not through bypassing—but through brutal honesty, energetic alignment, and the kind of radical self-responsibility that breaks the damn spell for good.

My Descent Into Obsession

I didn't fall in love—I fell into a trance.

It started like it does for so many of us: the signs, the synchronicities, the feeling like I had finally found "the one." The one my soul had been searching for across lifetimes. The one I was destined to reunite with. It felt like a divine collision—until it became a slow unraveling of everything I thought I knew about love, spirituality, and about myself.

At first, I called it destiny. I spiritualized the silence. I read energy into every text, every pause, every breadcrumb. I told myself this pain had a purpose, that the more it hurt, the more "aligned" we must be. I chased signs like they were oxygen, convinced that if I could just do more inner work, heal a little deeper, clear one more karmic block, then maybe—just maybe—they'd come back.

I was high on hope and drowning in delusion.

I spiraled. I obsessed. I lost sleep. I pulled cards three times a day and watched every twin-flame video I could find, only to end up more confused, more heartbroken, and more disconnected from the woman I used to be. My worth became tied to someone else's recognition. My intuition warped into anxiety. And my power? Gone. Leaking out through every unanswered message and every vision board plastered with their return.

I didn't just write this book. I bled it.

I burned for it. And I built myself from the ashes.

The Shattering That Became My Sovereignty

There came a moment when it all broke—when the fantasy cracked, and I could finally see what I had been avoiding all along.

I wasn't in love. I was in a trauma loop. I wasn't being spiritually tested. I was being spiritually hijacked—by my own unhealed wounds, my nervous system, my craving for someone to validate what I hadn't yet given myself. And that realization? It didn't feel like enlightenment. It felt like death. The death of the illusion. The death of the old me. The death of the girl who kept believing that if she loved hard enough, surrendered long enough, and held on just a little tighter… it would finally all work out.

But it didn't. And it wasn't supposed to.

The shattering came when I stopped waiting for "the one" to show up and realized it was me who had to rise. When I stopped asking for a sign and became the damn sign. When I stopped begging the Universe to bring them back and started asking myself why, I kept abandoning my own heart in the process.

That's when everything shifted.

Not overnight. Not in some perfectly packaged moment. But piece by piece—as I let go of the stories, the striving, the scarcity. As I faced the grief I had buried under "hope." As I stopped chasing someone who couldn't meet me, I started becoming someone who no longer needed to be found.

That's what this book is. The bridge between obsession and sovereignty. Between losing yourself and finally coming home.

What You'll Find in These Pages

I didn't write this book from a mountaintop. I wrote it from the floor.

From the dark nights, the obsessive thoughts, the collapsed nervous system, and the heartbreak that left me begging for clarity. But I also wrote it from the other side—after guiding thousands of men and women through this exact fire. I've spent over a decade helping people break this spell. Not just spiritually, but psychologically, energetically, somatically. And after witnessing this pattern in every form it takes—from the hopeful to the hysterical, the spiritualized to the downright self-destructive—I've come to one truth:

The twin-flame obsession isn't about a person. It's about a pattern. A wound. A mirror.

And once you see it for what it is, you can stop spiraling—and start rising.

I've written about this before. My first book on Twin Flames has been called everything from *"The Twin Flame Bible"* to *"The Roadmap for the Hottest Relationship of the Century."* And for many, it was exactly what they needed to make sense of the journey. It gave language to something otherworldly. It validated the signs, the connection, and the purpose. And I honor that work. I still believe in the power of the mirror, the sacred contract, and the awakening that happens through these connections.

But this book?

This is what comes *after* the awakening.
After the fantasy.
After you realize the real reunion was never meant to be with them—it was with *you.*

Twin Flame Obsession isn't here to romanticize reunion. It's not another cosmic pep talk telling you that they're "coming back if you just surrender harder." And it's definitely not a one-size-fits-all twin-flame manual written from the outside looking in.

This is about breaking the trance.

It's about reclaiming your energy from the endless spirals, the false hope, the future-tripping, and the emotional addiction we keep calling "union."

This book is part confessional, part spiritual detox, and part soul retrieval.

Inside these pages, you'll uncover:

- Why this connection feels so intense—and how it's wired into your biology, trauma, and soul blueprint
- How to stop chasing energetic breadcrumbs and call your power back
- The difference between divine love and emotional addiction
- Why letting go isn't failure—it's freedom
- How to shift from survival energy to magnetic alignment
- Tools to soothe your nervous system, reprogram your mind, and reset your energetic field
- And how to stop needing closure—because you become the closure

Each chapter includes personal stories, reflections, rituals, practices, and mantras designed to help you remember who the f*ck you are—and finally, come home to the love you've been looking for all along: your own.

A Message for the One Who Feels Like They're Losing Their Mind

If you feel like you're going crazy—you're not.

You're just waking up.

You're waking up to how much of yourself you gave away. To the years you spent calling it "unconditional love" when it was really unhealed hope. To the ache that no one else seems to understand because this isn't just a breakup—it's a soul rupture. One that shakes your body, your beliefs, your purpose, your entire reality.

You're not weak for still loving them. You're not broken for still checking the signs. You're not delusional for wanting it to mean something. It *did* mean something. It woke you up.

But now it's time to stop bleeding out in the name of growth.

This chapter of your story doesn't end with reunion. It begins with your return—to your body, your breath, your truth. To the part of you that never left. The one who knew, deep down, that love should never cost your sanity. The one who's rising now, even as everything else falls away.

Let this book be your mirror, your medicine, your map back home. You don't need to figure it all out. You just need to *choose yourself*—again and again, until you remember that you were never crazy.

You were just cracked open to finally see the truth:
You are the love you've been waiting for.

The Real Reunion Was Always With You

You didn't come here to chase love. You came here to *remember* that you are love. To wake up from the fantasy. To break the spell. To burn the version of you that begged for breadcrumbs—and rise as the version who builds their own table, sets their own standards, and becomes so full of self-worth that anything less than truth repels itself.

You came here to become the one you've been waiting for.

That's what this book will walk you through—chapter by chapter, layer by layer. Not just how to stop obsessing over your twin flame but how to *transmute* that obsession into power. Into clarity. Into magnetic sovereignty that calls in a love that actually meets you.

You're not here to keep spinning in the pain.
You're here to alchemize it.

And this time, you're not doing it for someone else by fixing yourself.
You're doing it by coming home to *you*.

So take a breath.
Say goodbye to the version of you who needed them to choose you.
And turn the page.

Because the reunion you've been craving?
It starts in the fire—right here—right now.

With fire, truth, and love,
Dr. Harmony

Part One

Caught in the Spell

CHAPTER 01

THE OBSESSION BEGINS

Why can't I stop thinking about them?

It wasn't just a crush. And it definitely wasn't a typical breakup. This was something deeper—something haunting. The connection felt cosmic, and sometimes, it still does. It was unlike anything I'd ever experienced. But what once felt divine had begun to consume me.

I found myself waking up with them on my mind, checking my phone for messages that never came, begging the Universe for signs—and then seeing those signs everywhere. There had been no contact in weeks, maybe even months, yet somehow, they never really left. I wasn't crazy. But I was entangled.

This was the twin-flame obsession. A spiritual bond so intense it *felt* like divine love—but behaved more like emotional addiction. It promised union but more often delivered confusion, despair, and the kind of soul spirals that make you question your worth, your sanity, and even your existence. I know because I lived it. And here's what I now understand: the very pain that overtakes your heart is the same pain that can set you free—if you let it.

Many people confuse obsession with love, particularly within the context of the twin-flame dynamic. The connection is explosive—magnetic, with uncanny synchronicities and a sense of cosmic destiny. But beneath all of that, something else is happening. Twin flames don't just awaken love. They awaken your deepest wounds. They mirror the parts of you you've yet to meet, to heal, to hold. And if those wounds stay buried—if the fear and pain go unacknowl-edged—the sacred connection mutates into a toxic cycle of craving and collapse. You're no longer reaching for love. You're trying to survive the ache of longing.

That's the trap. You start chasing—not because you're weak or des-perate—but because some part of you believes your twin flame holds the key to your wholeness. If they would just choose you, everything inside you would finally feel okay. But no one else can give you what you've been withholding from yourself. No text, no apology, no fantasy reunion can repair the places where you've emotionally abandoned your own heart!

This chapter is an invitation to go deeper. Together, we're going to look at why this obsession feels so spiritually significant and so chemically addictive. We'll explore the biology of trauma bonding, the emotional imprints left by your past, and the soul contracts that called this person into your life. You'll start to see how easily sacred love can disguise self-abandonment—and how quickly devotion can turn into distortion.

Because the obsession? It was never really about them. It was about the part of you that's still waiting to be chosen, the part that believes your worth depends on someone else, the part that forgot how powerful you truly are. That longing to be chosen, to feel wor-thy, to remember your power—that's what's been calling for healing all along. Not the connection. Not the relationship. But healing the wound underneath it.

When the Signs Aren't Enough

The signs were everywhere. Angel numbers followed me like shad-ows—11:11, 222, 717. *Every time I looked at the clock, it flashed back at me with a message I'd read as union, alignment, or divine trust.* Songs would play out of nowhere, echoing our story line by line. Dreams brought them back to life night after night, only to vanish again by morning.

I felt like I had been spiritually hijacked. Every moment felt like a message. And every message gave me just enough to keep holding on.

It felt sacred. Fated. I told myself, again and again, that I wasn't chasing "the one"—I was trusting the process. But the truth was harder to admit: I was spiraling. *I had stopped living in the physical world.* I wasn't grounded in my body or present in my own life. My energy was completely wrapped around them—their absence, their silence, their aura. And the signs? They weren't bringing peace anymore. They were feeding something inside me that was starving for clarity, certainty, connection... and, most of all, validation.

Then came the day—and night—that cracked everything open.

I had spent hours online, cycling through tarot readings, scrolling social media, pulling cards, meditating, and asking the Universe for answers. I told myself I was receiving divine insight, but really, I was just trying to soothe the ache. I hadn't eaten. I hadn't moved. I couldn't focus on anything except decoding the meaning of it all. My entire body was buzzing—not from alignment, but from depletion.

That night, I ended up on the bathroom floor. Lights off. Phone face down. My body curled in on itself, tight with exhaustion and grief. I wasn't just heartbroken—I was empty. And I realized I wasn't mourning a breakup. I was mourning myself.

In that stillness, something inside me gave out—not in weakness, but in surrender. It was like my soul let out a long, exhausted sigh. I looked up in the mirror and didn't recognize the woman staring back at me. I whispered, "What are you doing?" And in that single moment, everything became clear.

This wasn't love. It was obsession. And in the name of sacred connection, I had completely abandoned myself.

That moment became the turning point.

I realized the pain I'd been drowning in wasn't just about missing them. It was about missing me. I had left myself behind—my needs, my truth, my center—and I had been calling it unconditional love. I had been waiting for someone else to come home to me when I was the one who needed to return to myself. It was sobering. Humbling. And it marked the beginning of my reclamation.

No amount of signs, synchronicities, or soul contracts could justify how far I had drifted from my own soul. What I thought was devotion was actually emotional dependency dressed up in spiritual language. And it wasn't healing me—it was hollowing me out.

That night, I made a decision. I couldn't keep living in energetic limbo, holding space for someone who wasn't standing in it with me. I couldn't keep calling it surrender when it was really self-abandonment. The obsession wasn't proof of our bond—it was a mirror reflecting everything in me that still felt unworthy, unseen, and unloved.

And from that moment on, I began the long journey back—not toward them.

But back to me.

The High That Hurts: When Obsession Masquerades as Love

There's a reason this kind of love feels like nothing else you've ever experienced. It doesn't just touch your heart—it takes over your thoughts, overrides your nervous system, and settles into your soul like wildfire. From the very first encounter, there's often a profound sense of recognition. It doesn't feel like a beginning. It feels like a remembering. You don't just meet them—you remember them. That's when the ignition hits. Not a slow build but a cosmic eruption.

And while that eruption feels divine, it's also intensely chemical, emotional, energetic, and karmic.

What most people don't realize in the haze of that activation is that the high isn't just spiritual—it's biochemical. Your body floods with dopamine, oxytocin, and adrenaline. These are the same neurochemicals that bond us through both intimacy and trauma. Your brain starts wiring itself to that rush, and before you realize it, your body begins to crave the next hit of their energy. In that sense, the connection starts to mirror addiction. Over time, it's not even the person you're longing for—it's the version of *yourself* you felt in their presence. The way they awakened parts of you that had been dormant, silenced, or unseen.

Then comes the crash. *The silence.* The energetic withdrawal. And with it, the spiral.

You start searching for signs, replaying every memory, trying to decode their last message, hoping for anything that might bring back the high. But by this point, you're no longer responding to a person—you're reacting to a pattern. The more they retreat, the more your system clings to the fantasy. The deeper the void, the more vivid the illusion becomes. That's when obsession takes root—not as love, but as survival. You're no longer holding on to reality. You're chasing the imprint of what was.

This is where the twin-flame paradox becomes the trap. You tell yourself it must be sacred because it feels so intense. That it must be destiny because no one else has ever pulled you in like this. Every silence turns into a spiritual test. Every delay feels like divine timing. Every ache becomes an initiation.

But obsession isn't proof of love. It's a mirror reflecting your deepest, most unhealed emotional wounds.

What's really happening is the collision of soul recognition and trauma activation. This connection doesn't just show you who they are—it reveals every fracture still hidden inside you. The parts that ache to be chosen. The shadows still waiting for validation. The pain that never got the closure it needed. And in that chaos, you start to mistake the depth of your longing for the depth of the love.

But in reality, you're not chasing them. You're chasing the feeling of being safe, worthy, and whole.

That doesn't mean the connection wasn't real. It doesn't mean the twin flame wasn't a soul catalyst. *But if the price of that connection is your peace, your power, or your sense of self, then it's no longer love—it's a lesson.* Love doesn't demand your depletion. It doesn't hold your joy hostage or rewire your nervous system into a state of survival mode. Love liberates. It grounds you. It expands you.

Obsession does the opposite. It contracts, isolates, and drains you to the core.

Learning to distinguish between them isn't always easy. But it's necessary. Because naming the obsession for what it is—that's the first step in breaking the spell.

Why You Can't Let Go: The Chemistry of Soul Contracts and Trauma Bonds

You can feel it in your bones—this wasn't just another connection. There was something in their eyes that stopped time, a sound in their voice that felt like home, a pull in your chest that whispered, *This is it.* And maybe it was. But the deeper question is—*what exactly was it?* Because sometimes what feels like destiny is really a doorway. And not every doorway is meant to be a destination.

There's a reason you can't stop thinking about them, even when you know it isn't healthy. Even when your body is exhausted, and your spirit is heavy. It's not just about heartache. The twin-flame dynamic doesn't simply live in your heart—it takes root in your nervous system, your subconscious, and your soul memory. It imprints itself into your being like a sacred brand, pulsing with a frequency you can't seem to shake.

Let's be honest about the science of it. When that initial connection happens, your body responds with a flood of dopamine—the same chemical that fuels addiction. You feel high. Euphoric. Alive in a way you've never felt before. And then there's oxytocin—the bonding hormone. It's released not only through physical intimacy but also through emotional sharing, spiritual resonance, and even telepathic connection. The result? A full-body imprint that says, *I need this person to feel complete.*

But it's not just about chemistry. It's also about karma.

Often, the twin-flame connection arrives at the exact moment your deepest wounds are ready to be exposed. It feels like love—but it also feels like war. The same person who reflects your light also triggers your shadows. The same pull that awakens your soul also stirs your pain. Why? Because this isn't just a relationship. *It's a soul contract.*

These contracts are forged long before this lifetime, designed to catalyze growth, awakening, and deep remembrance. But many are rooted in unfinished stories—traumas you haven't yet healed, patterns passed down through your lineage, and emotional debts carried across lifetimes. That's why your twin flame often doesn't arrive as a savior. They come as a mirror. A disruptor. A divine trigger wrapped in the illusion of *"the one."*

And that creates the perfect storm.

You're facing a chemical addiction, a spiritual contract, and the resurfacing of unhealed trauma—all at once. Of course, you can't just "move on." It feels like something bigger is pulling the strings. The obsession isn't weakness—it's the byproduct of converging forces inside you. And it feels impossible to escape because part of you still believes that healing will come through reunion when, in truth, healing begins the moment you return to yourself.

This is the part no one tells you: *You can end the contract. You can release the loop. You can honor the love without being bound by the pain.* The chemistry can be rewired. The karma can be cleared. The power can be reclaimed. But only if you stop mistaking emotional intensity for soul alignment. Only if you stop calling chaos *confirmation.* Only if you stop chasing the version of love that keeps you stuck in survival.

Because what's hardest to let go of isn't actually them—it's the fantasy that they would rescue you. And once you stop needing them to save you, the spiral begins to unwind. Letting go isn't about rejecting the connection. It's about rewriting the meaning you've given it.

And in that space, there's finally room for you to come back to yourself.

Are You in Love or Just Obsessed? The Subtle Signs You're Caught in the Loop

It starts subtly. A tug in your chest. A name that won't leave your mind. You miss them, wonder what they're doing, and ask the Universe for a sign. And like clockwork, it appears—a license plate, a song, a dream. It feels divine like the cosmos whispering *'yes.'* As if you're on the brink of a great reunion. You tell yourself it's faith. You call it a soul bond, and you believe it's meant to be.

But slowly, quietly, something shifts. You're no longer just missing a twin flame—you're consumed. *Every thought loops back to their absence.* Every emotion hinges on their silence. Every spiritual tool you once used for grounding becomes a searchlight, scanning for evidence that they still care. Your energy is no longer your own. It's been overtaken by hope and reprogrammed to orbit someone who isn't here.

This is how obsession begins—not with chaos, but with a longing that wears the mask of love. And in the spiritual world, it's even harder to spot. We're taught that unconditional devotion is holy and that patience is proof of faith. But there's a difference between holding space and abandoning yourself. Between sacred connection and spiritual co-dependency. Between love... and obsession.

So, how do you know when you've crossed that line?

You know when your nervous system is constantly scanning—checking their feed, pulling another card, rereading old messages, asking your guides if this is still real. You know when your peace is held hostage by a question mark: *Will they come back? Do they still feel it? What does this mean?* You tell yourself you're letting go, but underneath the mantra is a motive: *Maybe they'll feel it. Maybe they'll notice. Perhaps this will finally pull them in.*

And that's where the pain sharpens. Because your spiritual practice—once a place of power—has now become a bargaining chip.

You're not meditating to meet yourself. You're meditating to manifest them. You're not journaling for clarity. You're journaling for a timeline. You're not healing to be free. You're healing to be chosen. It's not growth. It's spiritual self-abandonment.

Obsession doesn't always look frantic. Sometimes it's quiet. Patient. Polished. It sounds like trust, but it feels like an ache. It appears to be strength, but underneath, it's holding your breath, waiting for someone else to breathe life into you. And the truth is, the longer you sit in that space, the more disoriented you become. Because the more you pour your energy into them, the more disconnected you become from yourself.

You start shrinking. You second-guess. You override your body's signals in the name of "divine timing." And little by little, your own voice gets quieter, your boundaries get thinner, and your sense of self begins to dissolve.

But here's the truth you need to remember: the moment you start losing yourself to keep the connection alive... it's no longer sacred. Real love never requires your self-abandonment. A genuine connection doesn't come at the cost of your peace. If your worth, your wellness, or your truth has become collateral damage in the name of this bond—it's not love. It's longing. It's obsession. It's a loop.

And the obsession isn't a sign that they're "the one." It's a sign that you've lost touch with who *you* are. You're not here to chase clarity. You're here to *become* it. You're not here to wait for someone to return. You're here to return to yourself.

Because when you do? The loop ends.

The Ache Beneath the Chase: What You're Really Looking For

You think you're chasing them. That if they would just come back— if they'd apologize, awaken, finally see you—the ache would stop. The story would make sense. Your heart would settle. Your soul would exhale. You imagine that with their return, peace will follow. But what's really happening is that something deeper inside you is being stirred—something that's always been there long before they arrived.

It's the memory of being lit up. The moment you felt alive in your twin flame's presence. The way your chest opened like a flower, your heart skipped like it had just remembered something ancient and authentic. You became attached not just to the person but to what they represented. That rush of being seen. The glow of being chosen. The illusion that your soul had finally found its home. That feeling is what took root—not the reality, but the energy they awakened inside you.

And this is where obsession becomes so deceptive, especially in the twin-flame journey. It dresses itself in love, but underneath, it's often stitched with the wound of unworthiness. The connection doesn't just activate devotion—it ignites the belief that you must *earn* love to be enough. That if you're chosen, you're worthy. And the more they pull away, the louder that ache grows. Because now it's not just about love. It's about proving you deserve it.

But this isn't love—it's reenactment. A subconscious repetition of something old. Something familiar. Something you experienced long before they arrived. Maybe it was a parent whose affection came and went like a tide. Perhaps it was the lesson that love was conditional, presence was earned, and vulnerability could be met with withdrawal. Your twin flame didn't create the wound. They revealed it. They lit the torch and brought it to the surface, making it loud, vivid, and too painful to ignore.

That's why it hurts so deeply. Because when you grieve a twin flame, you're not just grieving the connection. You're grieving every time your heart reaches, and no one reaches back. Every time you lit up for someone who didn't stay. *Every time you whispered "see me" into a silence that never answered.* This grief isn't just about them—it's ancestral. Cellular. Patterned. And profoundly personal.

You believe you're longing for them. But beneath that longing is the deeper ache—the ache to stop abandoning *yourself* in the name of being loved by someone else. That's the real loss. Not their absence. Yours. The way you disappeared from your own body, your own truth, your own emotional center in the hope that their love would bring you back.

And that's what this obsession is here to show you. It's not a punishment. It's a portal. A doorway back to your own essence. A reflection that was never meant to consume you but to illuminate hidden aspects of yourself. You were never supposed to merge with the mirror. You were meant to *remember* the reflection is yours.

So if you find yourself saying, "Why do I feel this way?"—try asking, "What does this say about where I still believe I need love from someone else to validate who I am?" Because what you're really searching for isn't them.

It's you.

Breaking the Spell: Reclaiming the Power You Gave Away

There's a moment on the twin-flame journey where you realize you've built your identity around someone else's potential. Not who they are now, but who you believe they could be—if they healed, if they awakened, if they finally saw you the way you see them. You've been holding space not just for the connection but for a version of them that only exists in your imagination.

That's the spell.

It's not the person that has you trapped—it's the promise. The illusion that if you hold on long enough, love will finally redeem every wound. You start living in a future fantasy, making decisions based on a connection that isn't actually happening in real time. You justify the pain. You silence your own intuition. And little by little, you hand over your power in the name of devotion.

This is what no one tells you about obsession: it doesn't always feel desperate. Sometimes, it feels purposeful. Sacred. Even empowering—because you've convinced yourself you're on a spiritual mission. But when your worth is on the line, when your peace is constantly sacrificed to hold space for someone who won't meet you halfway—that's not the purpose. That's programming.

Reclaiming your power means calling yourself out with compassion and self-acceptance. It means being honest about the ways you've abandoned your own truth in service of their potential. About how much you've dimmed your light, delayed your healing, or distorted your boundaries just to keep the door open a little longer.

Overcoming obsession isn't about blaming yourself. It's about waking up. Because the real spell isn't love—it's the belief that your healing depends on someone else's return. And the moment you stop waiting for them to wake up... is the moment you finally do.

You don't need them to come back to move forward. You don't need closure to reclaim your clarity. You only need one decision: to stop giving your power away in the hope that someone else will eventually see your worth.

You see it now. And that's what breaks the spell.

The Reclamation Rituals: Grounding Truth into Action

Reading about obsession is one thing. Reclaiming your energy from it is another. This is where awareness becomes alchemy. Where the story you've been trapped in becomes the medicine you now carry. These rituals are more than practices—they are portals. Each one is designed to gently guide you out of the loop of longing and back into your own center. Not to forget the connection. But to remember who you are within it.

Let this be the beginning of your return—not to them, but to you.

1. What Am I Really Craving? — Self-Inquiry Reflection

This isn't about overanalyzing—it's about getting honest. Beneath the obsession is a deep desire, often disguised as love but rooted in unmet needs. Use these journal prompts to move beyond the fixation and reveal the emotional truth underneath:

- What feeling do I associate with this connection?
- When was the first time I remember feeling this kind of longing?

- What belief am I holding about what this person can give me that I don't already have?
- What am I hoping will happen if they come back?

Write freely. No edits. Let the page hold it all. This is not about shame—it's about clarity. The goal is not to stop wanting love but to give yourself the kind of presence you've been trying to receive from someone else. The ache is not your enemy. It's your compass. Follow it inward.

2. Energetic Recall Statement — Power Retrieval Practice

Sometimes, the simplest shift is the most profound. Stand or sit in stillness. One hand on your heart. The other on your solar plexus. Breathe deep and slow. Let the noise fall away. Then speak this aloud:

"I call my energy back from every place I have left it.
I release the story that my wholeness lives in someone else.
I come home to me—fully, freely, and without apology."

Visualize a golden light flowing into your body, returning to the places within you that have felt empty, fragmented, or forgotten. This is not just a declaration. It's a re-entry. Do this daily to reset your field and remember where your authentic power lives.

3. 24-Hour Obsession Detox — Pattern Interrupt Exercise

This is your practice in presence. In sovereignty. In choice. For the next 24 hours, make a sacred agreement with yourself:

- No checking their social media.
- No tarot pulls or energy readings about them.
- No twin-flame videos, messages, or decoding signs.
- No rereading old texts or replaying past conversations.

Instead, redirect that energy into your own body and life:

- Move. Dance. Breathe.
- Create something that lights you up.
- Journal. Cook. Rest. Be still.

- Spend time in nature or with someone who sees you now.

Then, reflect on how you feel. What arises when the pattern isn't fed? What clarity returns when you're no longer chasing meaning outside yourself? This is not a punishment. It's a pattern reset. And it may be the first time in a long time that you actually feel yourself again.

Affirmation to Anchor the Shift

"I am not chasing love—I am remembering that I am love.
I release the illusion of lack.
I reclaim the power I once gave away.
I return to myself—and that is enough."

Repeat this aloud. Write it on your mirror. Tattoo it on your spirit. Let it guide your choices as you step forward—not in fantasy, but in embodiment.

Because you were never meant to orbit someone else's light.
You are the flame. And now... you rise.

The Obsession Was Never About Them: Coming Home to You

You thought the obsession meant something sacred. That the depth of the pain validated the connection. That if it consumed you this much, it had to be real. But obsession doesn't prove love. It reveals the places within you where love has yet to fully take hold. What you've been calling longing was your soul's way of trying to return to itself.

Beneath every spiral, every sleepless night, every attempt to decode their silence, a more profound truth was rising. The obsession wasn't your failure. It was your awakening. It mirrored not just your desire but your disconnection. And while you may have thought they were the key to your healing, what you were really seeking was a return to your own power.

You weren't chasing them. *You were chasing the feeling of wholeness you experienced in their presence.* But that wholeness was never something they gave you. It was a reflection of something already alive within you—something that now asks to be remembered without needing someone else to mirror it.

This is what the obsession came to teach you. That your power does not live in your twin flame's return. It lives in your return. Back to your breath. Back to your truth. Back to the self you left behind in the name of love.

When you start choosing yourself, the obsession begins to soften. The loop loosens. The fantasy loses its grip. And something even more powerful begins to rise—your authentic self. Not fractured or unfinished, but whole, grounded, and sovereign.

Because what felt like an obsession was really your soul's way of guiding you back to yourself.

And now—you're finally listening.

CHAPTER 02
WHEN THE FANTASY FEELS LIKE FATE

*I thought it was destiny—but it was my wound
disguised as a sign.*

There's a difference between love and longing. Between divine connection and emotional attachment. Between a sacred soul bond and the storyline your mind created to soothe the ache. But when you're in it—when your heart is wide open, and your soul insists this is meant to be—it all starts to blend. It feels real. Fated. Inevitable.

This is where the lines blur—when past wounds and present emotions become so entangled, you can't tell if you're feeling a connection or reliving the pain.

Not because you're lost or naïve, but because the fantasy doesn't feel like fiction. It feels like home. Not because it is—but because it mirrors the ache you've carried for years. That ache is so deeply wired into your system that it convinces you that this is your person—when what you've really encountered is a reflection of what still needs healing.

This stretch of the journey isn't about the person. It's about the projection. The world you built in your mind. The timeline you got attached to. The future you imagined and the story you told yourself about how this love would save you. It's about the hope that felt like home—even when the actual relationship gave you nothing solid to hold onto.

And the hardest part? You don't always realize you're inside a fantasy until it starts to fall apart.

Because you're not just grieving someone—you're grieving what it could have been. The healing you thought it would bring. The closure you swore it would deliver. The version of you who believed everything would finally make sense if only the twin flame returned.

That's why it hurts so much. You're not just letting go of a person; you're letting go of a part of yourself. You're letting go of a dream.

But the longer you chase the illusion, the further you drift from yourself.

We call it a soul connection, but often, it's a younger version of you trying to rewrite the pain of not being chosen. We spiritualize the pain, call it divine timing, and convince ourselves it's all part of a sacred plan. But underneath it? There's a nervous system stuck in a loop, a heart waiting for someone else to bring the healing only you can give.

This chapter is about breaking the pattern of reclaiming your energy from projection and anchoring it back into truth. It's about seeing the difference between what was real and what was rescued.

Because healing doesn't begin when the fantasy finally comes true.

It begins the moment you stop abandoning yourself for it.

The Maze of Meaning: When the Fantasy Becomes the Teacher

It felt like I was chasing something sacred—something the Universe had promised but refused to deliver. Every time I thought I'd learned the lesson, completed the cycle, or cleared the karma, I'd find myself right back in the loop. Same ache. Same signs. Same silence. Sometimes, a different person, but always the same spiritual pattern. I told myself I was evolving. That I was trusting divine timing. That every breadcrumb was proof I was on the path. *But the truth?* I was circling a maze with no exit. And the deeper I went, the more disoriented I became.

At the time, it felt like surrender. Like faith. Like accepting what was and trusting it was meant to be. I wasn't even initially sold on the idea of being with this person—they weren't my type, and the connection caught me off guard. But the signs kept pointing me back. I stayed loyal to the idea that this was divine and that this person was my twin flame. I held onto every synchronicity as if it were a lifeline. I convinced myself this was destiny… until it wasn't.

What I didn't see then was that I had attached my healing to their return. I believed that if they came back, everything in me would finally make sense. Their presence would unlock the version of me I hadn't yet become.

Each person arrived like a storm, intense and undeniable, stirring something ancient in me. It felt like soul recognition like fate knocking at my door again and again. I didn't want to question it. I needed it to be real. I needed the story to mean something. Because if it didn't, I'd have to face the truth of what I had given up—how many times I had silenced my own needs, abandoned my center, and waited for someone else to choose me and make me feel worthy.

I tolerated the emotional unavailability. I excused the inconsistency. I spiritualized the suffering. I told myself that the more it hurt, the more sacred it must be. But I was the one creating the story. I was the one scripting meaning into silence, projecting depth into the distance, and building a fantasy because reality was too painful to face. I didn't want to let go. Because letting go meant grieving not just the person but the entire belief system I had built around them.

It wasn't about them. It was about what they represented. A chance to rewrite the past. A shot at finally being chosen. A dream that if someone like them could love someone like me, I'd finally be enough.

But the signs started to lose their sparkle. The silence became louder than the synchronicities. And eventually, I had to face the truth: I wasn't being guided. I was being triggered. Not by the Universe—but by the wounds I still hadn't healed.

The most painful moment came not when they ghosted. Not when the dreams stopped. Not even when I saw them with someone else. It came when I looked at myself and realized I didn't recognize who I had become. The woman I saw was tired. Empty. Unanchored. Not because of what they did but because of everything I had abandoned in the name of keeping the fantasy alive.

That was the beginning of the shift. I didn't exit the maze all at once. I unraveled gently. Breath by breath. Choice by choice. I began to see that each "twin flame" had been a mirror—not to my destiny, but to my disconnection. They were never meant to stay. They were meant to reflect the pieces of me still waiting to come home.

And I came home.

Not to a timeline, a label, or a future someone else would build with me. I came home to my body, my truth, my voice. I stopped calling chaos sacred. I stopped mistaking longing for love. I stopped waiting for someone else to return... because I had finally returned to me.

The Mirror, Not the Messiah

We don't fall in love with a person. We fall in love with the reflection they awaken—the possibility, the hope, the dormant part of us that suddenly sparks to life in their presence. They arrive and stir something ancient, a knowing that feels older than this lifetime, deeper than logic can comprehend. It's not just attraction—it's recognition. And in that moment, we think we've found the one. But what we've really seen is the mirror.

When we're disconnected from our own wholeness, it becomes all too easy to crown someone else as the source of our salvation. We don't just see who they are—we project who we need them to be. Their presence becomes a promise. *Their potential becomes a prophecy.* We write the future in our minds before the present has even had a chance to unfold. And when their actions don't align with the vision, we don't abandon the vision—we cling to it even harder.

I did this for years. Every magnetic connection became "the one." The twin flame. The soul contract. The final piece. I didn't just meet these men—I placed them on pedestals, assigning sacred meaning to every interaction, every sign, every synchronicity. It wasn't just a connection. It was a calling. And I was sure it had to lead somewhere divine.

But over time, I realized I wasn't seeing them clearly. I was projecting my unmet needs onto their faces. I wasn't in love with who they truly were—I was in love with who I hoped they would become. I had turned them into messiahs, holding them responsible for healing wounds they didn't even cause. I wanted them to prove that I was enough. That I was chosen. That I was worth staying for. And in doing so, I placed the weight of my healing on their shoulders.

What I didn't yet understand was that the connection wasn't meant to complete me—it was meant to reveal me. These men weren't my saviors. They were my mirrors. And the pain I felt when they pulled away wasn't just heartbreak. It was the collapse of the illusion. The collapse of the fantasy I had built to avoid facing the part of me still aching to be seen by my own eyes.

This is the danger of projection. It feels like faithfulness, but it's really deflection—away from our own truth, our own grief, our own unmet longing for love that never abandoned us. We think we're surrendering to destiny, but we're often just avoiding the discomfort of presence. Because to be present means seeing what's real. And sometimes, what's real is that the relationship only ever existed in our hopes.

But projection isn't a flaw. It's a form of self-protection. It's how our inner child tries to find safety. It's how we attempt to script a better ending to an old wound. And yet, the moment we become aware of it, we're offered something far more powerful than a fantasy—we're offered freedom.

Because once you realize you've been loving the mirror, not the messiah, you stop outsourcing your wholeness. You stop waiting for someone else to prove you're worthy. And in that moment, you begin to embody the very thing you were chasing. The love. The light. The truth.

And that's when the mirror loses its power. Not because they changed but because you did. You stopped looking to be saved—and started seeing yourself clearly, not as someone waiting to be chosen, but as someone who already holds the key.

Fantasy Bonding – Trauma's Favorite Love Language

Some bonds feel written in the stars but are actually etched in your scars. It feels like a connection you've waited lifetimes for. The chemistry is electric. The synchronicities are relentless. The dreams are vivid, the energy intense, and the emotional pull undeniable. Everything inside you screams, *'This is different.' This is it.* And maybe it is. But only if you're willing to tell the truth about what "it" actually is.

Because if you zoom out—if you were to step away from the signs and step into the present—you might see something else entirely. You'd see a pattern. An inconsistent person. A connection marked by more absence than presence. A dynamic that leaves you feeling more confused than clear. But you override it all because the dream of what it *could* be is more intoxicating than the reality of what it is.

That's the stronghold of fantasy bonding. You're not actually con-necting to the person in front of you—you're connecting to the story in your head. You build closeness not through shared experience but through projected meaning. You take moments—a text, a look, a memory—and turn them into sacred proof that the bond is real. You assign purpose to their silence. You tell yourself their absence is part of the divine plan. You craft an entire future around a rela-tionship that only fully exists in your imagination.

I've done it. I've clung to the signs, the symbols, the astral dreams. I've cried myself awake from visions I was convinced were sent by Spirit, believing that surely, he was feeling it too. That this was destiny. We were guided, timed, and chosen. But he wasn't there. Not really. He wasn't consistent. He wasn't communicating. He wasn't matching my emotional investment. And yet, I held on harder. Not to him—but to the idea of him. To the version of the story where it all made sense someday.

I told myself he was healing. Awakening. Clearing *karma.* That his distance meant he was feeling too much to say anything at all. I gave meaning to the silence. I turned breadcrumbs into confirmation. I mistook absence for depth. And every time I felt the ache of not being chosen, I dug deeper into the fantasy—because letting go felt like a failure. Because I'd rather keep hoping than admit I was loving alone.

That's the heartbreak of fantasy bonding. You become addicted to a closeness that doesn't actually exist. You keep loving someone who isn't choosing you, and you call it faith. You stay loyal to a possibility and abandon yourself in the process. Because somewhere deep inside, the longing feels familiar. And familiar feels safe—even when it hurts.

But there comes a moment when the fantasy stops feeling beautiful and starts feeling brutal. When the hope that once lifted you begins to drain you. When the love you thought you were keeping alive is actually keeping *you* from living. And in that moment, you face a choice.

You can keep spinning the story. Keep chasing the vision. Keep waiting for a chapter that was never promised. Or… you can open your eyes, look at what's really here, and come back to reality.

That isn't giving up on love. It's growing into it. It's understanding that fantasy isn't the path to fulfillment—presence is. And the moment you stop waiting for someone else to reflect your worth is the moment you begin to embody it.

That's when the real connection begins. Not with the dream. But with you.

Future Tripping & "Someday Syndrome"

There's a particular kind of ache that comes from loving someone who only exists in a version of the future you've imagined. A future where they heal. Where they awaken. Where they finally choose you. You tell yourself, *once he's ready, he'll come back. Once we're both aligned, everything will fall into place. Once she sees it clearly, we'll reunite.* And so you wait—tethered not to reality but to a timeline that hasn't happened.

I will be the first to admit it feels spiritual. However, we wrap the craziness in surrender, call it divine timing, and name it destiny. We even hold space and feel guilty for moving forward. And all the while keeping one foot in the present and our entire hearts in a version of tomorrow that keeps moving just out of reach. Insanity becomes a safe place—a sanctuary and a prison. You feel faithful. Devoted. Loyal. But beneath the surface, there's a quiet betrayal of self that begins to take root. Because what you're really doing is deferring your happiness to a later date, putting your peace on layaway, and sacrificing your present moment to a future you've scripted in your mind.

And the truth is, no matter how sacred it sounds, future tripping is just fantasy in disguise. It's your nervous system clinging to "someday" because "now" feels too uncertain, too painful, too real. It's the voice of your inner child saying, *Maybe next time it will be different. Maybe next time I won't be left.* But that next time never seems to come. And so you stay. You shrink. You spin. You build your life around a possibility and call it purpose.

I know this place too well. I lived in someday. I decorated it with rituals and reasonings. I told myself the delay was part of the design. That the waiting was my initiation. That I was being refined by the pause. But the more profound truth was that no one was asking me to wait. I had made that choice. I had bought into the myth that love meant endurance, that the longer I held on, the more deserving I would be of the ending I imagined.

But eventually, I had to face what was in front of me. Not in the fifth dimension. Not in astral dreams. Not in potential. In reality. And the reality was that they weren't showing up. Not now. Not here. Not in a way that honored the love I was holding. I had confused loyalty with self-abandonment. I had mistaken hope for guidance. I had wrapped my worth around someone else's future readiness instead of anchoring it in my own present truth.

That was the moment everything changed. Not because they came back or the vision finally manifested. But because I stopped waiting for someone else to deliver my destiny. I chose to become the version of me I thought would only exist once love returned.

And in doing so, I brought myself back from the edge of the illusion.

Not someday. Now.

Addicted to the Absence

Longing can disguise itself as love—especially when your nervous system is wired to equate love with distance. You say you miss them, but you've built walls around your heart so high that you're unconsciously afraid to open up to the depths of real love. What you're really chasing is the high. The dopamine hit. The rush of hope floods your chest when you think they might return. The sharp inhale when their name lights up your screen. The sting of a song that takes you right back to that one perfect moment. It feels like sacred love. But what you're actually experiencing is the chemical imprint of addiction.

Your body doesn't differentiate between soul connection and survival chemistry. It just responds. And when the connection is lit with intensity, your brain releases a cocktail of dopamine and oxytocin that mimics the imprint of deep attachment. You feel lit up, alive, whole. You feel seen. Even if it's only for a moment. Even if that moment lives more in memory than in reality. Then comes the silence. The absence. The sudden drop. The crash that follows the high. And in that crash, you find yourself spiraling—not just emotionally, but biologically.

You reach for anything that might recreate the feeling. You check their last seen timestamp. You replay old messages, old memories, old moments that made your heart believe. You scroll through their photos. You analyze dream meanings. You revisit a playlist you once built just for them. Not because you want to torture yourself— but because you're trying to stabilize the rush. You're trying to calm your system with the very triggers that keep it dysregulated. This circle of insanity is not just spiritual longing; it's a biochemical loop.

What does all this really mean? You are experiencing a trauma-bond dynamic in disguise. A cycle that feeds on intermittent rein-forcement—those moments of contact or hope that arrive just often enough to keep you hooked. The inconsistency becomes intoxicat-ing. The more distant they are, the more vivid the fantasy becomes. You convince yourself that the space is meaningful. That the ache is proof of a connection. That love is worth the waiting, the wonder-ing, and the unraveling. But if it only feels like love when they're not there—if your body is more lit up by the anticipation of their return than by their actual presence—then what you're feeling isn't love. It's withdrawal.

I used to live for the surge. I mistook the flutter in my chest for fate. I believed the butterflies were a sign of something deep and sacred. But they weren't. They were my nervous system replaying old wounds—patterns where love was unpredictable, affection was in-consistent, and I had to earn connection by being endlessly availa-ble, endlessly hopeful. I thought the tension was romantic. I thought the pain was part of the path. I thought love was supposed to hurt this much.

But love isn't supposed to be a high. Love is a resting place. A safe space. A steady frequency that doesn't disappear when the text stops coming. Love doesn't live in the adrenaline rush. Love lives in the regulation. In the stillness. In the truth.

And when I finally understood the biology of what I was experienc-ing—the chemical hooks, the emotional flashbacks, the addictive nature of longing—I realized I wasn't in love. I was entangled in a loop. A loop I could choose to step out of.

That's when everything began to shift. Not because the signs stopped, nor because the dreams ended. But because I stopped interpreting my craving as proof of destiny. I stopped romanticizing my dysregulation. I quit chasing a version of love that only existed in the highs and lows of chaos.

Because love isn't something you have to chase.

Love is what meets you in the moment and asks nothing in return but for you to stay. And real love—the kind that nourishes instead of drains—doesn't leave you aching for more. It reminds you that you are already whole.

The First Love That Never Chose You

Before there was them, there was someone else. Long before the obsession began—before the soul pull, the eye lock, the telepathic dreams—there was a quieter story written beneath the surface of your skin. A story that didn't start with romance but with survival. Not with a partner but with a parent. Someone whose love you craved more than anything. Someone whose presence you longed to feel but whose attention came in fragments, inconsistencies, or absence. Maybe they were emotionally unavailable, consumed by their own pain. Perhaps they were physically present but never truly attuned to each other. Maybe you were praised when you per-formed but ignored when you cried. Whatever the details, the im-print remained: love is uncertain. Affection is conditional. Being cho-sen must be earned.

That was the beginning of the ache.

And it didn't disappear when you grew up. It just dressed itself in new forms. Because when you met your twin flame, that ancient ache lit up like a flare. The connection felt cosmic, electric, other-worldly—but also eerily familiar. Like a memory you couldn't quite place. Your soul said yes, but your body whispered, "We've been here before." It wasn't just a love story. It was a reenactment. A soul-deep attempt to finally get the ending you never received. You weren't just falling for them. You were trying to finish a chapter your inner child had been stuck in for decades.

So you held on. Waited. Hoped. You gave them your light and called it fate. You endured their absence and labeled it purposefully. You spiritualized their inconsistency and called it divine timing. And when they didn't choose you, it shattered you—not just because they walked away, but because it reopened every old wound that whispered, "See? You're still not enough."

They weren't the source of the wound. Instead, the spotlight made it impossible to ignore. They reflected the part of you that was still waiting to be chosen, not as a punishment but as an invitation. An opportunity to follow the ache back to where it began—not to rewrite the past, but to reclaim the part of yourself you had to leave behind to survive.

Because healing doesn't come from finally being chosen by them. It comes from showing up for yourself in the moments you were once left behind. From holding the child inside who still believes love must be earned. From whispering, again and again, "You don't have to chase anymore. I'm here now. And I'm not going any-where."

That's the moment the spell begins to dissolve. That's when the fantasy becomes the teacher, not the trap. That's when the obses-sion loses its grip—not because they came back, but because you did. And suddenly, the twin-flame journey is no longer about trying to resurrect a fractured love. It's about finally embodying the kind of love you've always deserved.

Because when you stop chasing the one who didn't choose you and start becoming the one who always will, everything changes.

You no longer need to be chosen. You remember—you are the choice.

Breaking the Spell: Tools to Reclaim Your Presence

After months—or maybe even years—of being emotionally anchored in a fantasy, returning to yourself can feel like landing in a foreign place. The silence that once drove you crazy may now feel like space. The ache that once defined your day begins to soften, but not without resistance. That's how you know the spell is breaking. And in that threshold between illusion and embodiment, you'll need new tools—ones that don't pull you deeper into the loop but gently guide you out of it. These ideas aren't about forgetting the connection. They're about remembering your power.

1. Journal Prompts: Reality Check-In

The truth doesn't need to scream. It just needs a safe place to be heard. These prompts are meant to anchor you into clarity, not as punishment, but as liberation.

- What version of them am I holding onto that no longer exists—or never did?
- What can they give me that I haven't yet allowed myself to receive from within?
- How does my body feel when I imagine them versus when I remember the reality of their presence?
- Who would I be if I stopped waiting? What life would I create if I let go of the fantasy?

Let the words come without censorship. Trust what rises. This is how the truth begins to surface, and your power starts to return.

2. Pattern Disruptor: Rewrite the Story

The story you repeat becomes your reality. If you want a new outcome, you need a new script. Take a moment to write down the belief that's been keeping you stuck.

Old story: "We're meant to be, but the timing isn't right."
Now rewrite it in a way that reclaims your power:
New Truth: "I'm meant to be loved clearly, completely, and now. I don't wait for alignment—I embody it."

Read your new truth aloud. Speak it over yourself every time the old narrative tries to pull you back into longing.

3. Visualization Practice: Cutting the Cord to the future

Sit quietly. Close your eyes. Take a deep breath into your belly. Picture the future version of you—the one who stopped waiting. Not hardened, not closed, but radiant. At peace. Grounded in truth. Visualize yourself gently turning away from the illusion: not with bitterness, but with sovereignty. See the image of your twin flame as you projected them begin to dissolve, and feel yourself walk toward your fully embodied self—strong, centered, and present.

Now say aloud:
"I release the story. I return to my life. I reclaim my peace."

Let the energy settle. Let your nervous system feel the shift.

Affirmation to Anchor the Shift

Repeat this whenever the longing creeps in. Whisper it into your mornings. Speak it into your mirror. Let it become the truth your cells remember:

"I no longer wait for love—I become the one I've been waiting for."

When You Stop Waiting, You Start Living

Love that isn't grounded doesn't just hurt once—it haunts, first in the leaving, and then again in every moment you reach for something that was never fully there. You tell yourself it's sacred. That you're honoring a contract, holding space, trusting the process. But underneath the spiritual language is a quieter truth—your life has been on pause for a future that only existed in your imagination.

You didn't fall in love with them. You fell in love with the idea of what they represented. The one who would rescue you. The one who would return. The one who would finally choose you and make the ache make sense. Somewhere along the way, their awakening became the placeholder for your healing. Their love became the gateway to your worth.

The honest answer isn't in their return—it's in your remembrance. You were the missing piece all along.

They were the mirror. Yes. A sacred one. But they were never the destination—just the reflection. The turning point wasn't when they came in. It was when you stopped giving them the pen to write your story and picked it up yourself. When you stopped praying for their return and started preparing for your own.

That's when everything changes.

When you stop watching for signs, they might come back—and start tuning into the truth that you're ready to move forward. When you stop building a life around a "someday" and start living in the right now. When you realized their silence wasn't a test—it was permission. To breathe. To release. To rise.

The fantasy had a purpose. It gave you something to cling to while you rebuilt. It helped you survive. But now it's asking to be released. Not with regret but with reverence. Because it's no longer where you live.

You don't need to wait for love. You don't need to be chosen to be whole. You don't need to shape your life around someone who was never meant to stay.

This is where the story shifts. You are no longer the one who waits for the awakening. You are the one who wakes. And from this moment on—you live.

Fully. Freely. Now.

CHAPTER 03
MENTAL MADNESS

*I'm not crazy—this connection is just cracking
me open.*

The reminders were everywhere! Their name on a street sign, a stranger who looked just like them, a movie character with their voice, or a song that played during a moment I couldn't forget. And in an instant, I was back in the loop. It didn't matter how much time had passed or how certain I was that I'd moved on. One flicker of their energy in the world, and the spell reactivated.

My thoughts weren't just triggered—they were consumed. I'd find myself scrolling through old photos, replaying voice notes, and analyzing texts as if they held the missing piece. What started as love had become something else—tighter, darker, harder to name. A quiet obsession. Possessed. It felt like being possessed. I wasn't just remembering them. It was as though I was disappearing inside them.

This mental madness wasn't loyalty; it was mental captivity. A private war I kept waging—and no matter how many times I swore I was done, I kept losing.

Every part of me was reaching for something to hold onto, some thread of clarity in the fog. I searched the world for confirmation that what I felt was real. I studied passing conversations like they held secrets. I replayed dreams like they were maps. I scanned every moment for proof that the Universe hadn't forgotten me. But the more I chased meaning, the more untethered I became. I wasn't grounded in truth. I was floating in longing, losing pieces of myself with every unanswered question.

No one tells you this part of the journey. The same connection that cracks open your heart can also override your brain. That spiritual awakening can feel a lot like anxiety. Obsession can masquerade as intuition. You start mistaking the chaos for guidance, the pain for a sign, the madness for magic. But it's not. It's a pattern.

And if you don't see the pattern clearly, it will swallow you.

This chapter is about that pattern. The thoughts that persist. The compulsive need to decode everything. The way fantasy quietly turns into a fixation. It's where the twin flame stops being a mirror and starts becoming a trigger—not just for healing but for unraveling.

You're not broken. You're overloaded.

Moving beyond mental madness isn't about shame. It's about clarity. About recognizing that more information won't bring peace—because peace was never outside of you. The twin-flame journey isn't a riddle to solve. It's a story to rewrite. And it starts when you finally realize your mind was never meant to carry the weight of the connection. It was meant to serve your soul—not save it.

Freedom begins when you stop trying to figure it all out and remember that peace is never something you have to chase.

The Loop That Wouldn't Let Go

It didn't appear to be a loop at first. It looked like a second chance.

He wasn't the man I once believed was my twin flame, but the similarities were undeniable. From the moment we reconnected, something ancient stirred in me. He carried the same energetic signature—grounded yet chaotic, mysterious yet familiar. Both had recently ended twenty-year marriages. Both shared the same emotional intensity, the same spiritual vocabulary, and the same tender but unavailable presence. Even our connection mirrored the one before—only this time, it felt more embodied. More intimate. More real.

We had met a year earlier through a mutual friend. At the time, nothing came of it beyond a healing session. The timing wasn't right, but I felt a spark. I tucked it away, not expecting anything more. Then, almost exactly a year later, he reached out again—asking for another energy session. He was passing through town on business. But the timing, the tone, the undercurrent—it all felt too aligned to be coincidence.

I agreed to see him, and that one session became many moments. Emotional intimacy turned into physical connection. Something between us reactivated, but this time, it came with a weight. He was raw. Healing. In transition. He admitted he wasn't ready for more. He needed to focus on ending his marriage and rebuilding his life. He told me he had nothing to give—and as much as I tried to stay open and unattached, I felt myself getting pulled into his process. His confusion, timing, and emotional tides.

Eventually, I told him the truth: I was riding his waves, and in doing so, I was losing my center. I wasn't trying to pressure him, but the dynamic was too confusing. I couldn't go back to what we had before. I needed something clearer. More grounded. I needed to step out of the loop.

He picked me up and held me in his arms. He told me he never wanted to lose me, not even as a friend. Told me he cared enough to let me go if staying meant hurting me. I cried into his chest—not just over him, but over the painful familiarity of it all. The grief wasn't just about him. It was about watching the same story play out again and again, with a different face. The same dynamic, ache, and ending. Only this time, I saw it.

He eventually moved on. Entered a new relationship. Told me she reminded him of me—her energy, her eyes, her spiritual nature.

And I didn't fall apart. I didn't spiral. I didn't search for signs or explanations. Because something had shifted.

By stepping out of that loop, I had begun to see the pattern—not just in him, but in me. I saw how I kept attracting emotionally unavailable men who mirrored my own unresolved longing. I saw how I kept calling in connection that felt intense but unsafe. I saw how I was still hoping that someone else would choose me in all the ways I hadn't yet chosen myself.

That's when the healing deepened. That's when the spell started to break.

The more I chose clarity over confusion, peace over potential, and self-worth over self-sacrifice, the less I attracted people who couldn't meet me there. The pattern didn't repeat—because I no longer needed it to. I wasn't playing it out unconsciously. I was interrupting it on purpose.

It was never about blame, and it wasn't about regret. It was about finally seeing the pattern for what it was. The people weren't the problem. The ache wasn't the enemy. The chaos wasn't punishment. It was all information—reflections of the places in me that were still unconsciously waiting to be chosen, seen, and safe. And in that recognition, something in me shifted. Not all at once, but enough to change the course of everything. I stopped asking why they couldn't stay. I started asking why I kept inviting in people who could never meet me. Slowly, the obsession began to lose its grip. The cravings softened. The patterns that once felt magnetic began to lose their appeal. Because the loop didn't end when someone finally showed up and chose me. It ended the moment I chose myself—and meant it.

Prisoner of the Ping

The obsession doesn't always erupt in drama. Sometimes, it's much quieter than that—subtle, sneaky, and soft-spoken. It starts as a thought that simply won't stop. A ping in your chest the moment you wake up. A ripple in your energy field when their name floats through your mind. A low hum of awareness that clings to you no matter how full your calendar is or how busy your day gets. You're folding laundry, but you're also wondering what they're doing. You're chopping vegetables, but part of you is reliving a conversation from six months ago. You scroll past their name on a tagged post, and your entire nervous system lights up like it just received divine instructions. You check their profile "just once," and suddenly, it's two hours later, and you're down an interpretive rabbit hole, searching for meaning in an emoji or decoding the silence in their latest caption. You have a dream about them and spend the next morning dissecting every symbol, trying to discern if it was guidance or just your subconscious screaming for closure.

This isn't just overthinking. It's a full-body rehearsal for a reality that never quite arrives. You find yourself mentally rehearsing conversations that haven't happened, rewriting scenes that never played out, and emotionally investing in possibilities that exist only in your imagination. It's like your mind has become a stage—and you're performing every role. The Seeker. The Healer. The One Who Finally Gets Chosen. You're not receiving divine instruction. You're clinging to a mental simulation that feels safer than emptiness. And slowly, without realizing it, your intuition gets replaced with emotional forecasting. You're not present. You're not grounded. You're living in the echo of what you hoped this could be. It doesn't feel like fantasy. It feels like survival. Because if you stop running these scripts… what's left?

But over time, it begins to feel like a prison.

Because there's no end. No finish line. No breakthrough moment where the mental madness finally makes sense and brings peace. One ping leads to another. One thought breeds ten more. You go searching for comfort and end up suffocating in questions. I used to live for those pings—those energetic flutters that made me feel like they were thinking of me. Every time I sensed them, I'd abandon whatever I was doing. I'd freeze. Interpret. Decode. Obsess. It felt like intuition, like a soul tap on the shoulder. But what I didn't realize was that I was addicted to the rush. My nervous system had become hyper-attuned to their energy. Not because I was spiritually gifted—but because I was emotionally starved. I had learned to read the room before I could read myself. I wasn't grounded in truth. I was hooked on the high.

That's the real danger of staying in the obsession loop. You start mistaking hypervigilance for spiritual alignment. You call anxiety intuition. You mistake adrenaline for divine confirmation. Your thoughts stop being your own. Your peace gets put on layaway, waiting for the next ping to tell you how to feel. And slowly, without realizing it, you give your mind away to someone who may not even be thinking about you at all.

But a divine connection doesn't require overthinking. Love doesn't ask you to decode it. Your soul doesn't need you to chase clues. And if you find yourself mentally looping on someone all day, calling it alignment—it's time to pause. Time to ask: When was the last time I felt truly present? When was the last time I felt myself without reaching outside of me to feel it?

Because presence is peace. And the more you chase mental signs, the further you drift from your power. The thoughts will come. But they're not commands. You don't have to obey them. You can notice them. Breathe through them. And gently come back.

Because the pings aren't divine instructions. They're nervous system alerts. They're the body saying, "I'm still looking for safety."

And you? You're not here to be a prisoner to a thought loop that drains your life force.

You're here to reclaim the parts of you that were scattered by survival. To return to your presence, your power, and the truth that peace begins where you are.

The Addiction to Answers

There comes a moment on the twin-flame path when the goal quietly shifts. You don't realize it at first—it feels like growth, like soulful dedication. You tell yourself you're committed to your healing. That you're following guidance. That you're honoring the process. But beneath all of that well-meaning intention is something more desperate: you're no longer searching for love. You're searching for relief. You just want to feel okay again. You want the ache to make sense. You want the pain to mean something. You want something—anything—to quiet the chaos inside you.

Sometimes it's not clarity you're after—it's distraction. The constant thinking, analyzing, and decoding give your mind something to do. A job. A mission. A way to stay busy so you don't have to feel what's underneath. Because if you were to sit still for too long, you might have to face the silence. And the silence doesn't offer answers. It offers grief.

So instead of grieving, you reach. You reach for signs, for patterns, for timelines, for anything that will let you stay in motion. Not forward motion—just motion. Just enough to avoid the free fall into yourself.

The obsession becomes a placeholder. A way to stay tethered to something familiar, even if it hurts. Because letting go feels too much like disappearing. And you've spent so long anchoring your identity in this connection that you're not sure who you'd be without it.

But here's the deeper truth: The loop isn't always about them. Sometimes, it's about you avoiding the empty space they filled. The space that existed long before they arrived. The ache that has nothing to do with them at all.

And when you finally stop running from that silence—when you let yourself sit with the rawness of what's really there—you realize you're not searching for answers.

You're searching for yourself. Not the self who loved them. The one you abandoned trying to hold on.

But the high never lasts. Because you're not really looking for insight—you're looking for certainty. And certainty is a seductive drug, especially to the parts of you that were never taught how to feel safe in the unknown.

I used to believe that if I could just *understand* it all, I would finally find peace. That if I knew the timing, the lesson, or the divine plan— I could relax. But I wasn't seeking wisdom. I was seeking control. I was trying to manage the emotional chaos through spiritual logic. I consumed information as if it were medicine. But it wasn't soothing me. It was spinning me. The more I searched, the more disconnected I became—from my intuition, from my body, from my truth.

Because every message offered a new storyline. Every sign gave birth to a new theory. And every theory left me wondering if I was crazy or just not awakened enough to get it. The obsession stopped being about them. It became about decoding life itself—because somewhere deep down, I believed that if I could crack the code, I could earn my healing.

The truth is, the answers were never meant to save you. And no amount of readings, signs, or second opinions will ever give you what only your own presence can provide. Because clarity doesn't always come with certainty—and peace doesn't always come with a plan. Sometimes, it comes quietly. In the moment, you stop trying to figure it all out. In the moment, you breathe instead of bargaining. In the moment, you remember that intuition isn't a message you have to find—it's a truth that already lives inside you. And the day I stopped searching outside of myself for confirmation was the day I finally heard the only voice that mattered. Not from a sign. Not from a psychic. From within. And that voice didn't scream. It whispered: *You already know. You're just ready to live like it.*

The False Yes

There were moments when I was absolutely sure. Certain that what I was feeling was a sign. Certain that the sudden rush of energy meant they were thinking about me. Certain that Spirit was nudging me to just hold on a little longer.

My body would light up. My chest would flutter. I'd feel an electric charge that whispered, *'This is it.' They're coming back. Just wait.* And so I did. I waited. I watched. I surrendered. I aligned. I followed the breadcrumbs.

But the message didn't come. The call didn't happen. The reunion I swore I could feel never arrived. And I was left sitting in the silence, questioning everything. Was that really my intuition—or was that my anxiety, cleverly disguised as divine guidance?

One of the hardest lessons on this journey has been learning how to tell the difference between a soul-knowing and a trauma response. When you grow up learning to read the room, scan for danger, and anticipate emotional shifts as a way to stay safe, your nervous system becomes a finely tuned radar—and that radar often masquerades as intuition.

You start calling panic "downloads." You label emotional activation as "alignment." You interpret adrenaline as a spiritual message.

Real intuition doesn't feel like a cortisol spike. It doesn't flood your body with urgency. It doesn't come with a countdown clock or a desperate need to act right now; otherwise. That's anxiety. That's the inner child trying to predict pain so they can prevent it. That's survival, not spiritual guidance.

I learned this through many painful cycles—mistaking every rush of energy for a cosmic green light, every dream for a sign, and every energetic "ping" as proof. But when I finally got quiet—really quiet— I realized that the voice I trusted most didn't shout. It didn't clamor for attention or demand a reaction.

It whispered. It waited. It grounded me. It felt like peace.

It said things like *Let go now. Or This isn't your burden to carry. Or Your peace matters more than another heartbreak disguised as hope.*

That was my intuition. Calm. Steady. Rooted. It didn't need validation. It didn't need to be right. It just was.

And once I learned how to listen to that voice—the one in my gut, not the one spinning in my mind—I finally understood what it meant to be guided. Not pushed. Not panicked. Guided.

So if your "yes" is making you anxious, if your "signs" are keeping you hooked, if your "messages" are laced with fear and urgency—pause. Take a breath. Ask yourself if the voice you're following is really your soul... or your wound, doing everything it can to keep the story alive.

There's no shame in that. But there is a choice. And that choice begins with knowing that the real sign isn't the one that gets your heart racing. It's the one that helps you come back to stillness. Because peace is always the truth. And your clarity is the answer you've been looking for all along.

The Ending I Had to Write Myself

I used to wait for closure as if it were something only they could give, like the healing I needed, depending on their words, apology, or recognition of what we had shared. I convinced myself that if they just explained their feelings and acknowledged the connection, if they gave me some kind of validation—it would finally let me exhale. I fantasized about the moment it would all come full circle, the moment I'd feel seen, affirmed, whole. And so I waited. I kept the door cracked, both in my heart and in my energy, just in case. I clung to conversations in my mind, played out imaginary reunions, and kept one eye on the horizon of what might someday be.

But the longer I waited, the more I realized the pain wasn't just about losing them. It was about holding myself hostage to a story that no longer wanted to be written. The closure never came. The message didn't arrive. The full-circle moment never showed up. And that's when I understood the truth I'd been avoiding: they weren't going to be the ones to give me peace. They weren't coming back to rescue me from the silence they left behind. They weren't going to write the ending I was so desperately hoping for.

So I had to write it myself.

Not with a final conversation or a ritual soaked in symbolism. Not even with forgiveness—not at first. The closure didn't come wrapped in clarity. It came through surrender. I had to stop waiting for them to choose me and start choosing myself. I had to stop needing the story to make sense and simply let it be what it was: something sacred that didn't evolve into a relationship. A soul-stirring mirror that broke me open so I could rebuild from truth, not illusion.

It wasn't easy. My mind resisted. My nervous system grieved. My heart, for a while, still held out hope. But my soul began to soften. Because the moment I stopped waiting for closure was the moment I started reclaiming my power. I didn't need their words to make what I felt real. I didn't need a perfect goodbye to begin healing. I didn't need them to understand my pain to honor it; I just needed them to acknowledge it. The truth was always mine to hold.

Closure isn't something they give you—it's a decision you make. It's the quiet moment when you stop glancing backward and start building forward. It's the clarity that arrives not when someone returns but when you return to yourself. And that's what I did. I stopped saying "maybe." I stopped spinning in the fantasy of what could be. I closed the door—not with anger, but with peace. Not because the love wasn't real but because my healing mattered more.

I didn't have the final word. I didn't get the apology. But I had myself. My breath. My body. My truth. And that... that was more than enough.

Clearing the Noise: Tools to Reclaim Your Mind

Mental clarity isn't something you think your way into—it's something you choose moment by moment. These practices are designed to disrupt obsessive thoughts, calm your nervous system, and reconnect you with your own inner wisdom. This isn't about controlling your mind—it's about reclaiming your presence from the mental madness that's been running the show.

1. Journal Prompts – Releasing the Loop

Use these prompts to bring the subconscious spiral into conscious awareness. Let them create space between your thoughts and your truth.

- What thoughts am I looping on that I already know aren't serving me?
- What outcome am I still trying to control or predict through overthinking?
- What would I gain by letting go of needing to understand everything?
- If I stopped chasing answers, what would I have space to feel?

Let whatever rises be honest. You're not looking for the perfect answer—you're looking for what's real right now.

2. Pattern Disruptor – "The Thought That's Not Mine" Practice

When you catch yourself spiraling, pause and take a moment to regroup. Place one hand on your heart and the other on your belly. Breathe deeply and say out loud:

"This thought is not mine to carry."

Repeat it three times. Then ask: *What's true for me right now, in this moment?*

Let the answer be grounded. Your peace begins the moment you stop chasing mental certainty.

3. Nervous System Reset – Present-Body Drop-In

Obsessive thoughts often signal that your body is in a state of hypervigilance. This gentle practice helps return you to a sense of safety.

- Sit or stand with both feet on the ground.
- Slowly press each fingertip to your thumb, one at a time.
- With each breath, say silently: "I am here. I am safe. I am free."
- Continue for 60 seconds—or longer if needed.

Let your body lead the way back to presence.

4. Energetic Cut + Affirmation

When your mind is looping, speak this out loud while imagining the mental grip loosening its hold:

"I choose clarity over closure.
I release the need to figure it out.
I return to peace now."

Repeat as needed. Let this become your new anchor:
Peace doesn't live in the following answer. It lives in your next
breath.

Breaking The Mental Spell

There came a point where I stopped trying to untangle the web and started cutting myself free. Not with a dramatic goodbye or a sudden burst of strength—but with one honest question: "Is this helping me heal, or is it just keeping me occupied?" For months, I had been mentally looping in circles. Reading too much into every interaction, giving too much weight to things left unsaid, and exhausting myself with overanalysis dressed up as spiritual insight. But none of it brought me closer to peace. If anything, it pulled me further from my life.

The shift didn't come from another realization. It came from reaching my threshold. I was tired. Tired of outsourcing my worth to silence. Tired of chasing clarity from confusion. Tired of making a mental project out of someone who wasn't showing up. I didn't need more information. I needed my energy back.

And so I made a different choice. I stopped trying to prove the connection meant something. I stopped needing to feel right about what happened. I stopped waiting for the day it would all finally make sense. Because even if I never got a complete explanation, I could still choose to end the obsession. Not because I didn't care but because I was finally learning how to care for myself more.

This wasn't about indifference. It was about reclaiming my mental real estate. The spiral didn't break the moment I figured everything out—it broke the moment I realized I didn't have to figure it out to be free. The story didn't need a perfect ending for me to walk away with a clear understanding. It just needed to stop being the story I told myself every day.

Freedom didn't arrive with a message or a sign. It came in the quiet decision to put an end to the mental tug-of-war. To stop letting someone else's emotional availability determine my emotional stability. And in that choice, I found peace—not as a reward for figuring it all out, but as a result of letting it be what it was… and no longer making it my responsibility to fix it.

That was the thought that finally set me free.

Part Two

The Pain That Fuels
the Pattern

CHAPTER 04

WHAT YOU'RE REALLY CRAVING

I thought I wanted them—but I was starving for myself

There comes a point in the journey where it's not just about them anymore—but you're still hurting, and you can't figure out why. You've blocked them. You've pulled your energy back. You've done the meditations, the clearings, the cord-cuttings. And still... the ache lingers.

You keep thinking the pain is about the ending. About the way they left, about how love slipped through your fingers just when it felt like it had finally arrived. But what's hurting the most isn't just the loss of the person. It's everything their absence brought up.

It's not about the love that didn't last—it's about the impact it left behind.

The way it cracked something open in you. The questions it raised. The memories it stirred. The parts of you that it unearthed, which you hadn't touched in years, if ever. That's what still lingers. That's what still asks to be seen.

So what you're actually wrestling with isn't just a broken heart—it's a body that was never taught how to feel safe in love. It's a nervous system that confuses intensity with intimacy. It's a lifelong craving for something steady in a world that taught you love was earned through effort, performance, or pain.

You're not addicted to them. You're addicted to the spike. The way your system lights up with just one sign, one thought, one memory. It's not weakness—it's wiring. And the only way out isn't to shame the ache but to understand what it's really asking for.

This isn't about letting go of a person. It's about disentangling your identity from the chase. It's about noticing where the emptiness started long before they entered—and why their presence felt like it could finally fill it.

In this chapter, we will not rehash the heartbreak. We're going to excavate the root. We'll look at emotional addiction not as a failure but as a survival response. We'll examine the way trauma-trained love keeps you craving extremes—and how true healing isn't about detaching from them but reattaching to yourself in a way you never have before.

Because what you're really craving isn't closure. It's wholeness. Not peace through someone else. Peace inside your own skin. And for the first time—you're going to give it to yourself.

The Ache to Be Seen

For most of my life, what I truly craved wasn't just love—it was to be seen. Not for what I accomplished. Not for the image I projected. Not for how well I played the role others needed me to play. I longed to be seen for who I really was beneath it all—raw, real, whole. I wanted someone to look past the curated version of me and recognize the truth of my soul.

But that kind of love wasn't something I grew up knowing. In my family, love often felt conditional. To my father, I was a reflection of him—his pride, his legacy, his daughter, the doctor. When I aligned with that version, things felt steady. Safe. But the moment I began honoring my own truth—stepping into my voice, my gifts, my path—his acceptance became a currency I could no longer afford to pay.

I still remember giving him a copy of *Twin Flame Code Breaker*, hoping my words might build a bridge between us. That maybe, through my story, he would finally see who I had become. I found out two years later that he had thrown it away. And in that moment, it felt like he had discarded more than a book. *He had thrown away my soul.*

When I legally changed my name to Harmony—an identity I had carried in my bones long before it was ever written on paper—he told me he would disown me. And for a time, he did. Four months of silence. He deleted my number. Told others we had fallen out because I dared to believe that heaven wasn't some far-off place in the sky but something we could create here on earth through how we choose to live. He couldn't accept that. Because he couldn't accept me.

Until that moment, I hadn't fully realized how deeply his inability to see me had shaped every love story that followed. I kept unconsciously repeating the pattern—falling for people who loved the idea of me but not the reality of being with me. People who celebrated my light but couldn't hold my shadows. People were enchanted by my power, but they disappeared the moment I revealed my pain. And every time one of them pulled away, the same ache returned.

The ache of being invisible. The ache of being too much. Or not enough. The ache of the little girl who once stood in front of her father, heart wide open, shrinking just to stay in his field of vision. She didn't know she was dimming her light to be loved. But she learned. She learned that acceptance had to be earned. That authenticity was risky. That who she was at her core wasn't quite right. *Not safe. Not lovable.*

And so, without realizing it, I spent years chasing people who couldn't choose me. Because, on some level, I was still trying to rewrite the story with my father. I thought if I could finally be loved for who I was, maybe the little girl in me would feel seen. Validated. Worthy. But every relationship that failed to see me only deepened the ache.

Until one day, I stopped looking outward for that recognition. I stopped performing. I stopped bending, shrinking, and shape-shifting just to earn someone's attention. I saw the pattern, and I made a different choice. Not to shut down. Not to harden. But to end the betrayal of self that had masqueraded as love for far too long.

I chose to see me. All of me. The truth-teller. The healer. The little girl. The grown woman. The parts I had been waiting for someone else to acknowledge—I gave that recognition to myself.

And when I did, something shifted. The ache didn't vanish overnight. But it lost its power. Because I was no longer waiting to be seen. I was standing in the mirror, looking myself in the eyes, and saying, *"I see you. I love you. You are enough."*

And for the first time… I believed it.

The Root of the Ache

You weren't just missing them. You were missing the moment someone would finally stay. The moment someone would see *all* of you—not just the parts that were easy to love or aligned with their idea of who you should be—and say, *"I choose you. As you are."* That's what your heart was really aching for. Not just love, but presence. Not just connection but safety. You weren't just craving a relationship—you were craving reassurance that you were worthy of being fully known and still embraced.

And that's why this pain cuts so deep.

Because the twin-flame connection doesn't just ignite your heart—it awakens your history. It reaches into memories you thought you had outgrown, touches wounds you buried long ago, and brings every unresolved feeling to the surface. Every time, you felt invisible. Every time, love was withheld. Every time, you changed who you were just to be seen.

When a twin flame enters your life and reflects a version of wholeness you've never known, it feels like everything you've ever longed for is finally here. You don't just fall for *them*—you fall for the feeling of finally being met.

Until they pull away.

And then comes the unraveling. The sudden drop. The inner scramble to make sense of why something that once felt so right now feels like a void. But you're not just reacting to *this* moment. What's surfacing is the emotional imprint of every time love became unpredictable. Every time connection meant contortion. Every time, you felt like you had to shrink parts of yourself just to be kept.

Obsession is the impact of emotional abandonment. Your journey wires your nervous system to associate love with anxiety. With waiting. With proving and performing. It teaches you that connection is fleeting and that if you don't hold on tightly enough, love will vanish. And so you try harder. You adjust. You overgive. You become the healer, the good child, the high-vibe match—hoping that if you just get it *right* this time, they'll stay.

But all of that effort is rooted in an old wound. A deeper ache. You're not really trying to win this person's love. You're trying to rewrite the ending of the first love that left you feeling unworthy. You're reenacting the moment when someone taught you that your truth wasn't lovable—and you're still holding out hope for a different outcome.

Twin-flame obsession is real, and it's not a weakness. It's not desperation. It's the imprint of a nervous system that never got to feel safe… and a soul that never got to feel fully received. And now, here you are—once again trying to be enough for someone who may never have the capacity to truly see you.

But this time, the ending can be different. Because it was never really about them choosing you. It's about *you* choosing *you*. Selecting the version of you who stops hiding. Who no longer shape-shifts to earn love. Who releases the pressure to prove their worth. The one who wraps your arms around every part of yourself and says, *"I see you. I accept you. I love you. You're safe with me."*

That's what heals the root.
That's what ends the pattern.
That's what sets you free—for real this time.

The Real Addiction: Craving What Was Missing

What most people call "twin-flame love" is often something else entirely. It's not just about connection. It's not even about chemistry. It's about emotional hunger—a soul-deep craving that gets mistaken for destiny. That magnetic pull that feels like fate is often a flare from your inner child, finally getting a taste of the attention, intensity, and validation they've been starving for their whole life.

For a brief, shimmering moment, their presence quiets something ancient in you. That tightness in your chest begins to loosen. The unspoken ache softens. Their energy hits like medicine—because it gives you a glimpse of what you've always longed for. But that longing didn't start with them. It began in the places where you weren't met. In the moments, you had to become the strong one, the quiet one, the good one. The one who held everything together while no one noticed you were unraveling.

That's why the obsession feels so necessary. Because you're not just chasing a person—you're chasing the relief you felt when they first entered your life. You're chasing the possibility that this time, someone might finally stay. This time, you won't be left carrying all the emotional weight alone. You're not just drawn to who they are—you're drawn to how they made you feel: special, significant, chosen. Even if it was just for a moment.

When you grow up emotionally underfed—without consistent, attuned love—you learn to treat breadcrumbs like a banquet. You take what you can get. You stretch moments into meanings. You romanticize inconsistency and call it depth. You mistake longing for love. You confuse silence with spiritual space. You tell yourself the distance is divine, that the pain is proof of passion, that the absence must mean something holy is happening beneath the surface. But it's not sacred. It's survival. Because what they're feeding isn't your soul—it's your wound.

Emotional deprivation conditions you to tolerate relationships that trigger your earliest experiences of neglect. And because that ache feels familiar, it starts to feel true. You convince yourself you're being initiated. That it's all a spiritual test. That you're being shaped by some divine curriculum. But love doesn't require you to stay starving. Love doesn't withhold itself to teach you a lesson. Love doesn't disappear, and call it growth.

Real love nourishes. It fills. It shows up. It stays. And if you're chasing someone who leaves you more empty than whole, what you're experiencing isn't love—it's reenactment. You're not addicted to them. You're addicted to the hope that maybe this time, someone will finally give you what you never received.

But that healing isn't theirs to give. It's always belonged to you. And the moment you stop grasping for what was never stable and turn inward to meet the parts of yourself still craving to be seen, something shifts. Not because they changed but because you chose to become the one who finally shows up.

Why Your Twin Flame Triggers You So Deeply

Your twin flame doesn't just trigger you—they expose you. In ways you never expected. In ways no one else ever has. It's not about a missed text or a canceled plan. It's not even about the silence itself. It's what that silence awakens inside of you. Their absence doesn't just sting—it reverberates through every layer of your being, echoing through the cracks you've worked so hard to keep sealed. You don't just feel disappointed. You feel devastated. Not only because of what they did or didn't do but because of what their actions bring to the surface.

When they withdraw, it reopens the space where connection used to be—mirroring emotional gaps you've carried since childhood. When they go quiet, it taps into the memory of being ignored, misunderstood, or overlooked. When they withhold affection or presence, it brings you right back to the earliest moments when love felt conditional. You're not just reacting to them. You're reliving your history. And in that moment, they're not just a person—they become the embodiment of everyone who didn't see you, didn't stay, or didn't choose you.

They didn't create the wound. But they mirror it with precision. As if they were designed to match the very parts of you that still ache for closure. While your mind stays busy analyzing them, your soul is pointing inward, saying, *"Look here. This is the real reason it hurts."* Because the pain isn't new. It's ancient grief—surfacing with a new face.

That's why it feels so intense. You're not just longing for their love. You're longing for them to repair everything in your past that felt broken. You want their presence to be the redemption. The hope is that someone will stay this time. That this time, you'll be enough to hold.

They didn't come to finish your story. They came to show you where you stopped believing you could write the next chapter on your own.

Their presence peeled back the layers. Not to break you but to reveal what's still tender—what parts of you have gone unloved, unclaimed, or unspoken. The moments you silenced your truth just to be accepted. The times you withheld your needs because asking felt unsafe. The parts of you that never stopped wondering if love would only last if you kept earning it.

This was never about proving anything to them. It was about reclaiming everything you forgot belonged to you.

When someone mirrors your deepest wound, it can feel like a curse. But that mirror is sacred. Not because it reflects them—but because it shows you the pieces of yourself that are still waiting to be seen, chosen, and protected by you.

You don't need them to return to find closure. You don't need another conversation or a changed version of them to start healing. What you need is presence. With yourself. With your body. With your story exactly as it is.

Because the true shift doesn't happen when they come back. It occurs when you recognize that their purpose was never to complete you—but to reflect you. To awaken the parts you had tucked away. To trigger the wounds you were still carrying so you could finally tend to them. The ache wasn't just a loss—it was a mirror. And what it revealed wasn't a missing piece but a missing presence. Yours. The version of you who no longer needs to perform for love. Who no longer waits to be chosen. Who no longer searches for worth in someone else's eyes—because you've finally learned how to see yourself.

The Wound That Screams "I'm Not Wanted"

There's a specific kind of pain that hits when your twin flame pulls away. It's not just disappointment. It's not just heartbreak. It's a soul-level shattering—like something essential inside you has been ripped open and left exposed. And that pain runs deeper than the moment. It travels back through time to the first time you felt unwanted, unseen, or unworthy of staying.

Because that's what rejection does. It doesn't whisper. It screams. It screams through silence, delay, and the disappearing act. It screams when they look through you instead of into you. When you feel like you're too much and not enough at the same time.

This is the rejection wound—the one that says, *If they don't choose me, something must be wrong with me.* It's the voice that turns their silence into a verdict. It tells you their avoidance means you're unlovable, their absence proves you're invisible, and their emotional unavailability confirms you're broken.

But the wound you're feeling isn't new. And it's not just about them. It's the accumulation of every moment you were emotionally left behind. It's the memory of a parent turning away from your tears. The partner who ended things without explanation. The belief you quietly adopted was that you had to be smaller, quieter, or less of yourself just to be loved at all.

Now, your twin flame becomes the mirror for all of it—the one who touches the deepest, rawest part of your psyche and brings it into the light. And because the connection feels sacred as if it's destined, you don't just grieve the person; you grieve the connection. You grieve the possibility. The dream. The version of your future that felt just within reach if only they had stayed.

What's really happening isn't rejection—it's revelation. Something deeper is rising to the surface. You're not just grieving their absence. You're encountering the earliest imprint of what it felt like to be unseen. To reach for love and not feel it come back. This wound—the one that questions your worth, that quietly suggests you're too much or not enough—didn't begin with them. But their presence awakened it, making it impossible to ignore.

This isn't about them choosing someone else, either. It's about the part of you that's still waiting to be chosen by you. When you get this, everything begins to shift—not when they come back, but when you come back into remembrance of your own worth. When you stop using their attention as proof of your value and instead start meeting yourself with the love you've always needed.

When you truly let go, the ache begins to lose its grip—not because they changed, but because you did. You stopped abandoning yourself to keep a connection alive that was never meant to carry your healing.

Moving on isn't about loss—it's about redirection. An invitation to unlearn the idea that love has to be earned or chased. A call to break the pattern where pain becomes proof of devotion. And when you choose to answer that call—not with more chasing, but with compassion—everything softens. You stop running. You start listening. You stay.

And in that staying, something powerful happens: the wound finally gets what it always needed—not a partner to fix it, but your presence to embrace it.

The Lie That Keeps You Chasing

It's easy to think you're stuck because they won't choose you. But what really keeps the cycle alive is the part of you that keeps abandoning yourself to stay available for them.

You keep giving. Waiting. Hoping. Not because it feels good—but because, deep down, you still believe love must be earned. That if you try hard enough and stay long enough, they'll finally see your worth.

But overgiving isn't love—it's a form of self-rejection. A quiet sacrifice of your own needs in exchange for crumbs of validation. You're not stuck because of them. You're stuck because part of you still believes love should hurt to be real.

That belief turns longing into a loop. You chase approval, interpret silence as a test, and call emotional absence divine timing. You spiritualize the pain because it's easier than admitting that it doesn't feel like love—it feels like waiting.

And no matter how much you give, it never feels like enough. That's not because you're broken. It's because unworthiness repels the very love you're craving. The more you abandon yourself, the harder it becomes to receive anything real.

This isn't your fault. It's survival. A pattern built on early lessons taught you that love was something to earn, not something you simply deserved. But now, you see the loop for what it is—a reflection of what you still believe about yourself.

And the moment you shift that belief, even slightly, everything changes. You stop molding yourself to fit someone else's fantasy. You stop overexplaining your worth. You stop chasing closure, signs, or validation. Because you remember: the love you've been seeking was never theirs to give.

It was always yours to return to.

And when you start offering that love to yourself—without delay, without conditions—the pattern breaks. The ache softens. The wait ends. You stop trying to be chosen. And you start picking you. More importantly, you start living like you already are.

The Chase That Started in Childhood

The obsession didn't start with your twin flame—it started long before that. It began in childhood when you first learned that love wasn't always safe, available, or consistent. Maybe you had a parent who was emotionally present one day and distant the next. You were never quite sure what version of them would show up, so you stayed on high alert, scanning for cues, trying to earn their affection through behavior or silence. Perhaps you learned that achievement got you attention—straight A's, helping around the house, keeping it all together—so you began equating worth with performance. You believed that if you were good enough, responsible enough, quiet enough, maybe then you'd be loved fully.

You might have been praised for being strong but criticized for being sensitive. Or told to stop crying when your emotions felt too big. Slowly, you began to disconnect from your true feelings and started becoming who others needed you to be. Over time, your nervous system became wired not for safety but for survival—for reading the room, minimizing your needs, and bracing for withdrawal. Love started to feel more like a reward than a right, and chasing became the only way you knew how to stay connected.

Then someone walks into your life and stirs something profound. A connection that feels magnetic, familiar, and intense. They show up, then pull away. They see you, then disappear. And instead of walking away, you find yourself pulled in even deeper. You call it chemistry. You call it fate. But what you're really experiencing is your childhood pattern reactivated. You're not just longing for *them*. You're longing to rewrite the story you've carried for years—the story where you had to earn love to feel seen and safe.

So you try harder. You wait longer. You give more. Not because it feels good but because it's what you've always done. But this time, the pattern isn't just painful—it's showing you something important. It's not a test to pass or a contract to complete. It's a signal. A chance to heal the root.

You no longer have to chase. You no longer have to shape-shift or perform. What you needed then—presence, safety, unconditional love—is something you can begin giving yourself now. And the moment you do, the cycle can no longer continue. Not because someone else changed but because you no longer need to repeat the past to feel worthy of love.

Reclaiming the Craving: Tools to Break the Pattern

This work isn't about stopping the obsession through willpower. It's about listening to what it's actually asking for—and giving yourself the love that part of you never received. These tools are designed to bring you back to the center of your own love story. To help you move from emotional hunger to emotional nourishment. From waiting to remembering. From chasing someone else to choosing you.

1. Journal Prompts: Returning to the root

Let your pen become your truth-teller. Write without filters, just feeling your way back to clarity. Ask yourself:

- What do I believe I need from them that I don't believe I can give myself?
- What past relationship or memory does this ache remind me of?
- How did love feel in my childhood home—was it safe, consistent, conditional, earned?
- What version of myself am I abandoning when I chase them?

2. Emotional Reset Practice: Reparent the Ache

Close your eyes and take a slow breath in. Bring to mind the younger version of you—the one who first felt unseen, unwanted, or unworthy. Maybe they're five. Perhaps they're fifteen. Picture them clearly. Imagine kneeling down beside them. Let your present-day self take their hand. Feel your heart open as you speak these words aloud or silently:

"You are not too much.
You are not invisible.
You are not broken.
I'm here now.
And I will never leave you behind to chase love again."

Let your breath deepen. Let your body soften. Stay there as long as you need. You're not just imagining something—you're rewiring something.

3. Affirmation to Anchor the Shift

Say it. Feel it. Repeat it as many times as you need—especially when the urge to chase creeps back in:

> *"I no longer chase love to fix a wound. I give myself the love I've always craved."*

This is how you break the pattern. Not by force—but by finally giving the craving what it was always asking for: you.

The Wound Was Never the Problem—It Was the Portal

For so long, I believed my craving made me weak. That the depth of my longing meant something was wrong with me. I thought if I could just stop needing so much—stop needing to be seen, to be chosen, to be loved with consistency—I'd finally be free. But I was wrong.

The ache wasn't my flaw. It was my compass.

I wasn't asking for too much. I was asking for something I'd never fully received: to be held in my wholeness. To be loved not for what I could fix, produce, or perform—but simply because I existed. Because I was worthy, just as I was.

The obsession, the spiral, the hunger—they all came from the same place. A place in me that had been left unseen. Unmet. Unfed. And instead of judging her, I finally chose to sit beside her. To listen. To soften. To understand that the wound I had spent so long trying to escape wasn't a flaw—it was a message. A mirror. A portal back to the parts of me I had abandoned just to survive.

Because the journey was never about them. It was never about being chosen by another. It was about coming home to the truth that had always been buried beneath the pain: I was already whole. Already worthy. Already loved.

That's what ends the cycle—not their apology. Not their return. Not their sudden realization of what I meant to them. What ends the cycle is the moment you stop waiting for someone else to see you—and choose to see yourself instead. When you stop searching for rescue, remember: you are the one you've been waiting for.

The wound was never the barrier. It was the initiation. The sacred threshold. The exact place where the healing began. And once I stopped resisting it, once I stopped trying to earn what was already mine, I didn't need to chase anymore.

Because the truth was never in their validation. It was in that moment I finally remembered:

I was never too much.
I was never not enough.
I was never meant to be chosen.
I was meant to rise.

And now... I do.

CHAPTER 05
TRAPPED IN THE TRAUMA LOOP

Why does pain feel like love... and chaos feel
like home?

When love feels like survival, it doesn't just hurt—it short-circuits your entire system. One moment, you think you're okay—or at least pretending well enough. Then something shifts. A message goes unanswered. Their energy fades. The silence grows heavy. Suddenly, your stomach drops, your chest tightens, and your whole body braces for impact. It's not just sadness. It's a full-body shutdown. A nervous system flare so sharp it feels like something inside you is unraveling—and no one around you can see it.

You try to do everything you think is right. You block them. You journal. You light candles and whisper affirmations you barely believe. You sit in meditation and beg your breath to make it stop. You tell yourself you're strong, spiritual, and conscious. But your body doesn't respond to logic. It spins. It searches. It panics. Your mind says, "Let go," but your cells are screaming, "This isn't safe."

That's when the truth begins to crack through: this isn't just heartbreak. This is survival mode.

The twin-flame connection didn't just spark emotional pain—it activated every unprocessed trauma your body has carried. The part of you that learned love was anxiety. That connection was unpredictable. That desire meant danger. And from that place, your nervous system loops—desperate for contact, chasing a feeling of relief, mistaking adrenaline for alignment, or fearing fate will never arrive.

This is the trauma loop. The space where love and threat become indistinguishable. Where silence feels like abandonment. Where obsession isn't just emotional—it's physiological. It lives in your wiring, in your body's memory. So if you've ever wondered why you couldn't stop thinking about them, even after all the inner work you've done—it's not because you're weak or broken. It's because your body was conditioned to perceive love and pain as the same thing.

This chapter isn't about fixing you. It's about freeing you.

You're not here to suppress your reactions or spiritually bypass your feelings. You're here to understand them. To finally see that what looked like weakness was really your body protecting you. Your nervous system wasn't malfunctioning. It was doing what it learned to do: anticipate loss, prepare for absence, and armor itself against pain.

Now, we begin the work of untangling those patterns. We'll explore how survival responses became misidentified as love, how trauma shaped your perception of connection, and how to return to safety—not just in thought, but in your body.

Because you were never crazy. You weren't needy. You weren't broken. You were surviving a kind of love that never felt safe. And now—it's time to build a love that does. Starting with the love you give yourself.

When the Body Breaks So the Soul Can Rise

I had built an identity around not needing anything. I was the strong one. The space holder. The healer. The one everyone else leaned on. I trained the world to believe I would always be okay—and for a long time, I was at least on the outside. But when I wasn't, no one knew what to do with me.

It started with a short trip—less than 24 hours—to celebrate my dad and brother's birthdays. My brother had just gotten sick that day. I drove home, thinking nothing of it. But within three days, I was flat on my back with COVID. The initial symptoms seemed minor—fatigue, a sore throat, some brain fog—but I had no idea that this virus would become the spark that ignited an entire soul collapse.

My voice disappeared. Completely. I couldn't speak—and it didn't return for four months. When it finally began to come back, it was shaky and unreliable. It would come and go for over a year and a half. Even now, it sounds different. Not broken—just changed. It carries something new. An energy rooted deeper in truth. In fire. In everything, I survived.

But back then, I was coming undone. I didn't sleep for ten nights. Not a single minute. I couldn't eat. I couldn't shower without collapsing. I couldn't brush my teeth without my heart pounding. My body would tremble if I stood for more than a few minutes. My mind couldn't form thoughts. I was dizzy. Weak. Terrified.

Then came the panic. Full-body panic attacks, relentless and unexplained. My nervous system went into total collapse. It felt like my body was burning from the inside out. Every sound pierced me like knives. My heart raced. My breath disappeared. There was no off switch. I wasn't just reacting to COVID-19—I was responding to everything I had ever carried but never allowed myself to release. This was trauma looping on every level, not just from that moment—but from my entire life.

I went to the ER three times. The fear pulsing through my body felt like death. Eventually, they prescribed a narcotic I'd never taken before—just to give my system a chance to rest. Even then, it only gave me four hours of sleep before the spiral began again. I had no strength. No tools that could reach this level of collapse. I was depleted—mentally, physically, energetically, spiritually. And still, no one around me truly understood what was happening.

I asked my brother if his son could help me for a few days. That one request sent a ripple of panic through the family. People I hadn't spoken to in months began reaching out. My kids were called. My ex's family. Friends I hadn't leaned on in years. And without telling me, they found what they thought was a psychiatric facility. It turned out to be a drug rehab center. Their plan? Drop me off.

And I went. Not because I believed something was wrong with me—but because I needed help. I needed a safe place to land while I took the medication. I needed to be witnessed. Held. I needed someone to see what was really going on—not a breakdown, but a full-system shutdown. A total collapse of everything I had ever used to hold my life together.

My saving grace was a neighbor who didn't just drop me off at the ER—he stayed with me. He even slept on my futon for a couple of nights, keeping watch while I took the medication they prescribed—something strong enough to supposedly knock me out for hours. But even then, I only managed a few broken hours of sleep. And when I woke, I felt even worse. Disoriented. Heavier. Like the small flicker of relief I was promised had only deepened the fog.

Thank God, I met a psychiatrist there who understood trauma. She saw through the symptoms and gave me highly addictive medication to calm my nervous system—something I had always avoided. And I took it. Not to escape but to return. I stayed on it for 18 months. I never abused it. I never took the full dose. I prayed over it and used it as a bridge—because I wasn't trying to numb myself. I was trying to live. To survive. To find my way back to a self that could finally rest.

I didn't just feel broken—I felt hollow. Something inside me had collapsed, and in the silence that followed, my soul began calling out for refuge. I remember telling a close friend, "I can feel someone coming in—and whoever it is must be one hell of a person. Because for me to be this open, something deep is shifting." Overnight, I went from not fully knowing what it was like to feel alone to not knowing how to survive alone. And in that raw, exposed space, something unexpected happened.

Someone arrived.

Not with grand gestures or intensity but with a calm presence. He felt like medicine. Gentle. Grounded. Loving. He saw me. Walked beside me. Held my hand when I could barely stand. He reached parts of me I didn't even know were still aching. And for a moment, I truly believed—maybe this is it. Perhaps this is the reward. The sacred mirror. The divine partner I had cleared all this space for.

But love isn't linear. Because as I began to rise, he began to unravel. His trauma surfaced. His fear took over. His capacity to hold me faded. Emotionally, he disappeared, even while physically still there. And just like that, I was back in the trauma loop.

Only this time—I saw it. He didn't put me there. He just touched the part of me that still believed love and suffering were intertwined. That being seen always came with a cost. That if I let someone in, I'd have to pay for it later.

I spiraled. Again. But I didn't collapse. Because I wasn't the same woman anymore. This time, I didn't wait for someone to save me. I came for myself. I spent the next two years rebuilding—not just from COVID, but from the decades of trauma I had buried underachievement, independence, and spiritual bypassing.

I reclaimed myself. My truth. My nervous system. My peace. And now I see it all clearly: I had to lose my voice to find my truth. I had to collapse to stop carrying what was never mine. I had to meet him—not because he was the one, but because he was the mirror that showed me what still needed to be healed.

This wasn't a punishment. It was a preparation. Not for union with him—but for union with me. And now, I live from the stillness. I speak from the fire. And I carry a kind of peace that only comes when your soul has survived the storm.

Because I didn't just make it out.

I made it home.

When Love Feels Like Survival

People will tell you to just move on. To let it go. To stop thinking about them. To get over it already. But they don't understand what you're really up against. Because this isn't just about a person—it's about a pattern. A pattern that was etched into your nervous system long before your twin flame ever entered the picture.

The twin flame didn't cause the chaos. They exposed it. They activated the part of you still wired for survival—the part that had learned to equate love with longing, unpredictability with passion, and pain with proof that something was real. So when they appeared—then disappeared—when the connection became intense, then confusing, your system didn't interpret that as a red flag. It interpreted it as home.

What you're experiencing—the spiraling thoughts, the emotional whiplash, the crushing lows followed by euphoric highs—is not because you're broken or weak. It's not because you're not healed enough, not spiritual enough, or doing something wrong. It's because your nervous system is trying to survive something it never had the chance to process safely.

You were wired to repeat, not release. Your body is doing what it was designed to do: seeking out the familiar, tracking the threat, and chasing after whatever once looked like connection. If your earliest experiences of love were inconsistent—affection that came and went, a presence that turned into an absence—then that pattern became your normal. Not because it was healthy but because it was known.

That's why when they go silent, it doesn't just hurt—it torments. It floods your system with cortisol. Your chest tightens. Your thoughts race. Your breath shallows. And suddenly, it feels like your body is under attack. Because to your nervous system, it is. This is what the trauma loop does. It doesn't distinguish between danger that is present and danger that is remembered. It simply recognizes the signal and fires the alarm.

And the more this loop repeats, the more it reinforces itself—like a scratched record stuck on the same line. Your body learns that this pattern, this pain, this ache is what love feels like. The skipped track becomes your obsession. The fixation becomes your identity. And you find yourself looping around the same person, the same dynamic, the same emotional landscape, over and over again.

So no, you're not crazy. You're not too much. You're not "addicted" in the way people assume. You're dysregulated. You're in a trauma loop that love didn't create—trauma did. And you cannot think your way out of it. You cannot logic yourself out of a response that lives in your body. You can't meditate your way out of a nervous system that has been on high alert since you were a child.

The twin flame didn't break you. They mirrored the part of you that already felt broken. And that mirror is the beginning of the shift. Because once you stop asking, *"How do I fix the connection?"* and start asking, *"What does my body need to feel safe again?"*—everything changes.

Healing won't come from a union. It comes from regulation. From calming the internal signals that still believe love equals pursuit. From soothing the inner child who panics every time love feels like it's leaving the room. From teaching yourself that love and safety are not opposites—they are meant to coexist.

You weren't meant to survive love. You were meant to feel safe inside of it. And that safety starts now. Not with them. But with your body. Your breath. Your here. Your now.

Addicted to the Spike: When Intensity Becomes the Illusion of Intimacy

It wasn't just that I missed them. It was the anticipation that gripped me. The constant emotional suspense of not knowing what would happen next. Would they reach out today? Would they ignore me tomorrow? Would I wake up to a message or another wave of silence?

That uncertainty became its own kind of intimacy. And somewhere along the way, unpredictability started to feel like closeness.

When you never know what's coming, you're always paying attention. Hyper-focused. Tuned in. The edge becomes your baseline. The waiting becomes the ritual. The absence becomes the evidence that something meaningful must be happening beneath the surface—because how else could something feel this consuming?

But this is how trauma tricks us: it conditions us to equate intensity with importance. Not because the connection is soul-deep but because the instability mirrors something old. Familiar. And the body leans in, not because it's safe—but because it knows how to survive chaos better than stillness.

Soon, you stop asking, "Is this good for me?" and start asking, "Why hasn't it happened yet?" You stop measuring love by how it feels—and start measuring it by how often it hurts. The more confusing it becomes, the more convinced you are that it must be meaningful. And that's the conundrum: you keep holding on, not because the bond is growing—but because your sense of self is shrinking.

The spike isn't love. It's hypervigilance. It's emotional whiplash that leaves you addicted to being on edge. Because if love has always been a moving target, you've learned to keep running. To keep guessing. To keep proving that you're worth the hit of attention that arrives just before it disappears again.

But that's not a connection. That's survival dressed up as romance.

And when you finally stop running… when you stop scanning for signs and soften into the quiet… you begin to realize something profound: It was never about the next message. It was about finally breaking free from the part of you that believed inconsistency was love.

When Chaos Feels Like Chemistry

At first, it feels like passion. Your heart skips when they look at you. Your breath catches when they pull away. Your entire body lights up when they reappear after days of silence. You call it chemistry.

You call it fate. You tell yourself it's divine. But what if your body is telling a different story?

What you think is love might actually be adrenaline. What feels like a connection could be cortisol. That aching tightness in your chest—what if it isn't longing but a full-blown stress response? You say you "can't breathe without them," but your nervous system isn't writing a poem. It's signaling danger. And what you've been calling destiny… might actually be dysregulation.

Especially if you grew up in a home where emotional safety was scarce. Where love had to be earned. Where the rules were unspoken, and the consequences were invisible but heavy. If affection came wrapped in tension, if silence followed vulnerability, if presence always teetered on the edge of disappearing—then your body learned to associate love with uncertainty. With chaos. With contraction.

And now, as an adult, that same body doesn't always distinguish between connection and activation. Between intimacy and instability. Between someone who genuinely supports your peace—and someone who mimics the unpredictable patterns of your past.

So when someone is hot-and-cold, emotionally inconsistent, or just unavailable… you don't walk away. Your system bonds. It lights up with recognition. *This feels familiar.* And your body interprets familiarity as safety—even when it isn't. You start mistaking the spike for alignment. The highs and lows become your evidence that something meaningful is unfolding. The chase becomes your comfort zone. The longing becomes your compass. And all the while, your body is whispering that something is off—even as your mind keeps calling it love.

But real love doesn't spike your cortisol. It doesn't leave you gasping in silence or decoding mixed signals. It doesn't make you shrink to stay connected. Real love grounds you. Softens you. It invites your breath to deepen, your shoulders to drop, and your heart to stop bracing for impact. It feels steady—not because it lacks passion, but because it doesn't require panic.

I didn't know any of this at first. I thought the ache meant depth. I thought the tension meant truth. I believed the inability to relax around them was just part of being "spiritually activated." But one day, I asked myself a different question—one that changed everything:

Does this person feel safe in my body... or does my body feel like it's bracing for impact?

That question shattered the illusion. It stopped me from chasing the chaos. It helped me see that what I had been calling chemistry was really a trauma response. That my attraction to emotional intensity wasn't divine—it was deeply conditioned.

Because I wasn't created to survive love. I was made to rest inside it. To exhale into it. To let my nervous system feel the kind of safety it never learned was possible.

And so were you.

When It Feels Fated, but It's Actually Familiar

Not every powerful connection is meant to last. And not every soul-deep ache is evidence of divine love. Sometimes, what feels like destiny is really déjà vu—a familiar pain replaying itself, dressed in cosmic clothing. It doesn't arrive to complete you. It arrives to wake you. Not to fulfill a sacred contract but to expose an old wound, calling for closure.

You tell yourself this is your twin flame. That you've met for a reason. That this is karma, divine timing, or soul recognition. But what if it's not a soulmate you're responding to? What if it's a cycle? What if the pull isn't sacred—it's patterned?

Some bonds feel magnetic not because they're destined but because they *replay* what your body has learned to crave. The push and pull. The rupture and repair. The high of being seen and the low of being forgotten. It doesn't just feel familiar—it feels necessary. Not because it's safe but because survival taught you that inconsistency was love.

And if you've done the spiritual work—if you've studied soul contracts, practiced unconditional love, and believed in divine reunion—then you're even more likely to mistake nervous system chaos for cosmic confirmation. You hold on. You wait. You call it transformation. You call it the mission. But what if the real mission isn't about staying?

What if the lesson is in finally recognizing the pattern... and walking away?

This is the trap of a trauma bond: being magnetized to someone who activates your oldest wounds and soothes them just enough to keep you coming back. It doesn't feel manipulative. It feels intense. It feels real. But it's not built on safety—it's built on activation. And your body, wired for survival, doesn't yet know the difference.

You think you're chasing love, but you're really chasing the spike. That nervous system hit when they text you out of nowhere. That momentary relief is followed by a more resounding crash. And even though it hurts, even though it drains you, you stay—because, on some level, it feels like home.

But there's a difference between what's familiar and what's aligned.

Trauma bonds are fueled by repetition. By the chemical highs and lows of intermittent connection. They're not about love—they're about fear. The fear of being alone. The fear that if you let go, it means you failed. The fear that if you walked away, the connection wasn't real. So you keep calling it sacred, even as it costs you your sanity, your peace, your center.

But real soul bonds don't pull you out of yourself. They bring you back home. They don't leave you gasping in silence or chasing clarity. They don't spike your anxiety and call it chemistry. They regulate you. They soften you. They remind you that you don't have to earn love through pain.

Both kinds of connections can feel powerful. But only one leads to peace.

So if your heart is constantly spiraling in self-doubt, if your nervous system is always on high alert if you've done more inner work trying to keep the relationship alive than you've done to feel safe in your own body—then maybe it's time to ask the deeper question:

Is this sacred love... or is this just old soul patterning in a romantic disguise?

Your body will always be drawn to what it knows. And if what it knows is pain, it will chase pain—until you interrupt the loop. Until you reclaim your breath. Until you stop spiritualizing suffering and start choosing peace as your new divinity.

Yes, the bond may have been real. Yes, it might have awakened something inside you. But that doesn't mean it's meant to last. Because just as sacred as that meeting was, so is your right to leave. To protect your heart. To stop handing your peace over to someone who hasn't yet learned how to hold it.

Staying in pain isn't a spiritual achievement—it's a reenactment. You can honor the connection without sacrificing yourself to it. You can carry the love while laying down the chaos. You can let go—not because it wasn't deep, but because *you've gone deeper.*

Letting go of what's familiar, even when it feels fated, isn't giving up.

It's growing up.

And that decision—to stop confusing activation with alignment, to stop calling pain your path, and to finally come home to peace—that might be the most sacred act of love you ever make.

The Blueprint You Didn't Choose

Your body remembers everything—not just the heartbreaks or traumas, but the instructions it was given about love. Before you ever had the words to describe the connection, you were learning what love felt like through sensation and response. You learned through energy, silence, and tone. You learned through how long it took for someone to pick you up when you cried, whether your voice was welcomed or shut down, whether your needs were met with attunement—or annoyance.

And if what you learned was that love could vanish without explanation, that affection had to be earned, or that being yourself came with consequences, then your nervous system didn't just notice it—it adapted. You developed a blueprint. Not because you were broken but because you were wise enough to survive. You became what others needed: the helpful one, the easy one, the overachiever, the one who never asked for too much. You kept the peace, swallowed your pain, and made yourself smaller than your soul. And your body learned to equate love with vigilance, attention with performance, safety with silence.

When someone entered your life and truly *noticed* you—when their presence felt attuned, alive, even tender—it awakened something you hadn't realized was waiting. A quiet longing tucked deep beneath the surface. Not for the person but for the feeling of being seen, chosen, and valued without effort. For a moment, it felt like healing. But when they pulled away, when the connection became inconsistent or suddenly vanished, the reaction inside you wasn't just emotional—it was physiological.

Your body responded before your mind could catch up. You couldn't focus. Simple tasks felt impossible. You lost your appetite for food, for conversation, for life itself. The world dimmed like someone had turned the volume down on everything but the ache. And it wasn't just about this person. It was the resurfacing of every moment you had to disconnect from your own needs to stay connected to someone else. This wasn't just emotional pain—it was a cellular memory of every time you had to go invisible just to feel safe.

This process wasn't about losing *them*. It was about being thrust back into a nervous system that learned, long ago, to brace for the goodbye.

And you weren't just missing them. You were revisiting every time you felt emotionally left behind. And that's why it feels so overwhelming—why no affirmation or spiritual insight seems to touch the ache. You see, this isn't just a mental obsession. It's a physio-logical reaction. Your body is trying to protect you using the only model it's ever known. It doesn't understand that the chaos is no longer love. It still thinks unpredictability means connection.

Therefore, no matter how many cords you cut or how many mantras you whisper, nothing will shift until you stop trying to fix the person and start tending to the pattern. Because as hard as it is to admit it, this isn't about them. It's about what your body still believes it has to endure to be loved. Until that belief is updated—not just intellec-tually but also somatically—you'll continue to reenact it. You'll con-tinue to feel drawn to those who reflect it. You'll call it fate when, really, it's just familiarity.

When you finally have had enough, you no longer turn against your-self for craving love. You're turning toward the part of you that's been holding this blueprint alone for far too long. You're tracing the ache, not to a twin flame or a text thread, but to a childhood memory that never had the space to resolve. You're meeting the version of you who needed consistency and got chaos. Who needed presence and got pressure. Who needed love and got a checklist.

And that's where the shift begins.

Not by silencing your desire but by listening to what it has been trying to say. Not by rewriting the past with someone else but by rewriting the way you show up for yourself.

Because no—you didn't choose this blueprint. But you get to choose the healing. You get to choose what safety feels like now. You get to choose to stay with yourself in the moments you used to run. And in doing so, you don't just change your story.

You change your life.

Rewiring the Chaos: Tools to Teach Your Body a New Way

Healing the trauma loop doesn't start in your head—it begins in your body. You've likely exhausted every spiritual tool you know. You've read the books, recited the affirmations, reframed your thoughts, and tried to rationalize your way out of the pain. You've told yourself it's time to move on. You should have gotten over it by now.

But no matter how much clarity your mind claims, your body still holds the charge.

That's why we don't just need insight—we need grounding. Your body doesn't respond to what you know—but to what you feel.

You may not have chosen the original blueprint. And you didn't ask for love to be laced with anxiety. But you do have the power to change how your body responds now. These suggested practices aren't about controlling your emotions or forcing yourself into calm. They're about teaching your body—gently, consistently, over time—that safety is possible. That peace is allowed. That you no longer need chaos to feel alive.

Each tool below is designed to provide your body with a unique experience of love. One that doesn't spike your cortisol or send you into a state of survival. One that doesn't demand you chase to feel worthy. Just one breath, one choice, one moment of staying with yourself at a time.

1. Journal Prompts: Conversations with Your Body

Let these prompts invite you into dialogue—not just with your thoughts, but with your sensations. Allow your hand to move freely. Let your nervous system speak. Write without editing.

- What do I feel in my body when I don't hear from them?
- When was the first time in my life I felt that same sensation?
- What story does my nervous system believe about love, abandonment, or silence?
- What part of me still thinks I need chaos to feel alive?

These prompts aren't about finding the correct answers. They're about connecting with the part of you that's been silently carrying the weight. And now is where the release begins.

2. Somatic Practice: The Touch-Back Breath

This is not just breathwork—it's a return. A way to signal to your system that this moment is safe, even if it doesn't feel like it yet.

Place one hand on your heart. The other on your belly.
Close your eyes.
Inhale slowly for a count of four.
Hold for four.
Exhale gently for a count of six.
As you exhale, say:

> *"I am safe to feel.*
> *I am safe to stay.*
> *I am safe to be with me."*

Repeat this cycle three times—or more. Use it anytime you feel the spiral start. When your thoughts race, when your chest tightens, when your fingers hover over the old thread. Let this become your touchstone—not to bypass the pain, but to stay with it in a different way. To remind your body: *This isn't danger. This is a new story now.*

3. Affirmation to Anchor the Shift

Let this be your daily reorientation—a steadying voice in the moments your old pattern tries to pull you back into the spike.

> *"I release the need for chaos.*
> *My nervous system now chooses calm."*

Say it when you wake. When you reach for your phone. When you feel the ache swell in your chest. Say it when you feel shaky, uncertain, or tempted to reach for the pattern you've already outgrown.

You're not saying it to manifest magic.
You're saying it because *you are* the magic.

This is not about pretending to be healed. It's about creating conditions where your system can finally trust that peace doesn't mean punishment. That calm isn't abandonment. That safety doesn't mean silence.

Because what you're doing isn't just healing a loop.

You're building something brand new inside yourself.
A home.
A rhythm.
A relationship with your body is rooted in stillness, sovereignty, and self-trust.

And the more you return to it, the more your body starts to believe it.

Not because it's easy.
But because you've finally remembered—you are worth the safety you never received.

And now, you're learning how to give it.

The Loop Wasn't Love—It Was a Cry for Safety

You don't need another message to feel whole. You don't need a final sign, one more synchronicity, or a text that finally says what you always longed to hear. What you really need—what your body has been whispering, then screaming, then collapsing to express— is safety. Because what you thought was love... was often your nervous system locked in a loop, clinging to the only kind of connection it knew how to recognize.

That's the truth most people miss.

It wasn't just about missing them. It was about missing yourself— the version of you that once felt calm in your skin, anchored in your breath, at home in your body. But when your blueprint for love was built on unpredictability, when affection was conditional, and presence came with pressure, your body learned to call chaos chemistry. You weren't just chasing a person—you were chasing the illusion of safety through someone else's energy. Trying to patch a lifetime of unmet needs with brief moments of emotional relief.

And when they disappeared, when the silence returned, when the connection felt just out of reach again—your system did what it was designed to do. It panicked. It spiraled. It clung. Not because you're broken but because you never got the chance to learn another way.

I know this because I lived it. When I lost my voice, when my nervous system collapsed, and the world felt too loud, too much, too fast—when I could barely breathe or eat or think—I wasn't just grieving the person who had walked away. I was grieving all the years I spent calling suffering a soulmate. I was grieving every version of myself that believed pain was the price for love. That silence meant sacred. That staying in pieces would someday make me whole.

But the real healing didn't happen in a moment of reunion. It happened in the quiet. In the breath, I stayed with instead of abandoning my needs. In the mornings, I chose to show up for myself before checking in with their energy in the stillness, where I finally stopped reaching out—and started reaching in. That's when I knew I was no longer trapped in the loop. Not because the triggers stopped—but because I stopped running from them. I started listening to what they were really saying: *Please make me feel safe.* And for the first time in my life, I did.

You're not too sensitive. You're not too much. You're not broken. You're patterned. And patterns can be rewritten. That spiral isn't your shame—it's your signal. It shows you where your body still believes love must be chased to be kept. But now? You get to choose something different. You get to stay with yourself when it hurts. You get to become the source of the safety you've always needed.

This is your moment. Not when they return. Not when the karmic lesson is finally complete. But now—right here—when you decide to stop abandoning yourself for someone who was never meant to save you. Because the real reunion isn't with them.

It's with the part of you that's been waiting for peace. And peace was never going to come from them. It was always waiting inside *you.*

CHAPTER 06
FACING THE FEAR OF LETTING GO

If I let go… who will I be without this story?

Let's be honest. Letting go of your twin flame doesn't just feel hard—it can feel impossible. It's not just closing a chapter. It feels like tearing away a piece of your own soul. Like cutting off your oxygen supply. Like walking away from something cosmic, sacred, and destined—something so profound, no one else could possibly understand it the way you do.

But underneath all of that intensity, there's something even more gripping than the loss itself—fear. Not just fear of heartbreak, but the kind that whispers questions you don't dare speak aloud. *What if this was your only shot at real love? What if no one else ever makes you feel this way again?* What if you finally let go… and they come back just after you've moved on?

The fear isn't really about them. It's not even about the relationship. It's about what they symbolize. The mirror. The answer. The breakthrough. The cosmic connection that was supposed to make all your pain make sense. They became the one who would finally prove that your love was powerful enough, loyal enough, unconditional enough to rewrite the ending.

So you stayed. You surrendered. You waited—sometimes in silence, sometimes in spirals—because somewhere inside, you believed the ache would be worth it. That the reunion would redeem the pain.

But at some point, that pain becomes heavier than the hope. At some point, your body stops confusing devotion with depletion. At some point, your soul begins to whisper a different truth—not about losing them, but about finding you.

Because the real grief isn't about them disappearing. It's about you realizing you've been disappearing, too. Waiting to be chosen. Hoping to be rescued. Delaying your joy until someone else decides you're worthy of it.

Letting go doesn't mean the connection wasn't real. It means the version of you who needed the connection to feel real is ready to evolve.

And that's what this chapter is about: the moment you stop holding on to the illusion and start holding yourself. The threshold where grief ends, and power begins. Where identity unravels and freedom rises. Where you stop chasing the love that hurt you... and start attracting the love that heals you.

You're not giving up on love. You're giving up on the version of it that required your suffering to prove it. And in that surrender—not defeat, but sacred release—you begin to remember who you were before the fantasy... and who you're becoming beyond it.

I Stopped Fixing What Wasn't Mine to Fix

I remember the moment I realized I wasn't just letting go of *him*—I was letting go of every outdated version of me that I thought I needed to hold on to.

After my divorce two decades ago, I spent four solid years rebuilding from the ground up—doing the deep work, healing my wounds, and facing my patterns. I didn't know anything about twin flames at the time. All I knew was that I wanted to call in my soulmate.

Someone aligned. Conscious. Ready. And when he arrived, I truly thought I had.

For four years, it was heaven. We built a life that felt sacred. He showed up in ways no one ever had. It felt safe. Steady. Beautiful. However, the cracks soon began to appear. The connection that once felt effortless slowly turned into a quiet, exhausting battle. What followed were three years of hell—emotional disconnection, unspoken resentments, and a slow erosion of the foundation we had built. Still, I stayed an extra year. I was determined to see if we could find our way back.

But he had already checked out—mentally, emotionally, and spiritually. And I, like I had done in every relationship before, began bending. Fixing. Trying to do the work for both of us. I convinced myself that if I just healed one more thing, if I just softened one more wound, I could pull us back into alignment. It was like forcing a square peg into a round hole, refusing to accept that it no longer fit.

What hurt the most wasn't losing him. It was watching myself disappear again—shape-shifting into the version of me that tolerated too much, gave too much, and held on too long. That version of me had worked so hard to be chosen. But in doing so, she had forgotten to choose herself.

Each person I attracted after that mirrored a new version of me— an upgraded reflection of my growth. They each carried a piece of me but never the whole. Some taught me clarity. Others cracked me open. One felt like a spiritual storm. Another, like a familiar lullaby. And then there was *him*—the one I called the pencil to my Etch A Sketch. He helped draw all my fragments together, not to complete me but to show me the picture I hadn't been able to see: I was never missing anything. I just needed to remember the wholeness that had always been there.

But even with him—the man who made me feel seen in ways I never had—I had to let go. Because sometimes, even the best connection becomes misaligned. And staying in something that once felt right, just to preserve what *was*, only prolongs the pain. The ache wasn't just about losing the relationship. It was mourning the loss of the self I had outgrown—the one who still believed that love had to be earned through endurance.

Letting go wasn't a one-night awakening. It wasn't some dramatic declaration. It was a thousand small moments of release. Like finally exhaling after years of holding my breath. Like watching a balloon float upward after realizing I'd been clutching the string in fear.

And with every layer I released, I met a new version of myself. Not the one who needed someone to validate her light—but the one who could finally stand in it.

Letting go didn't mean the love wasn't real. It meant the lesson was complete. And the most sacred thing I could do wasn't to stay in the story—but to honor the chapter for what it gave me... and begin writing a new one from the truth of who I'd become.

The Death of Who You Were Becoming
Letting go doesn't just feel like a loss—it feels like death. But not just the death of the connection. The death of who you became inside it. You built an identity around this relationship. You were the one who held space, believed in divine timing, forgave endlessly, stayed soft in the ache, strong in the storm, and faithful to the signs. You became the version of yourself who believed—believed in the love, the soul contract, and the sacredness of the pain.

So when it finally came time to let go, it didn't just feel like walking away from them—it felt like walking away from who you thought you had to be to keep the love alive. That version of you—the one who clung to hope and waited for the full-circle moment—was still holding out for rescue. Still hoping that love would be earned if you just held on long enough. Still aching for something that felt like home, even if it hurt.

That's why it was so painful. Because what was dying wasn't just the dream of reunion—it was the version of you that had poured everything into the fantasy. The person who believed they needed to be chosen to feel complete. The one who gave their power away in exchange for the possibility of being loved in return. And as heart-breaking as it was, that death was sacred. Because what was dying wasn't the real you. It was the performance. The programming. The layers of yourself you had built just to feel worthy.

And underneath it all, there you were—the one who never needed to be rescued. The one who was always enough. The one who had been waiting for *you* to choose yourself.

Letting go of this identity caused a kind of grief I didn't know how to name. I could feel it in my bones—an actual mourning of who I had been. I knew I needed to honor that version of me. She had carried so much. She had loved so deeply. She had given everything for the dream.

So, I turned it into a healing ceremony. I set the intention to celebrate the parts of myself that I was releasing. I wanted to bring light to the sides of me that had gone unseen. To say goodbye to her with reverence, not shame. I asked a friend to write my eulogy—not for my death, but for the death of my old identity. I wanted to hear how someone else saw me. What they witnessed in me that I hadn't acknowledged in myself.

What she wrote cracked me open:

> *"You are exemplary in never-ending faith and trust. Even when your days have felt dark and your nights alone, you have navigated your way through it with your inner compass. No matter how deep the waters have felt where you had to tread to keep yourself afloat, you have always swum yourself back to shore. A candle in the wind that never blows out.*

> *You have taught others by showing them unconditional love and loving in the way you want to be loved. Nothing less. You have lived a life without projecting judgment. You've fought against your vulnerabilities only to discover the strength within them and embrace your own, as well as those of others. You have high standards, but never place them on anyone else. You've always seen the silver lining in everything.*

Your generous spirit and unwavering belief in love are what books could one day be written about. You live your story like a fairy tale—always believing, always giving, always hoping. Even when you feel pain in every cell of your emotional body, you have more to give from your cup of love. May that cup always and eternally be overflowing. You will leave your energetic imprint on every soul you have touched and loved."

I wept when I read her words—not just because they were beautiful, but because they mirrored back parts of me I had never truly seen. I felt honored. Witnessed. Loved. And something inside of me softened. For the first time, I was able to fully grieve who I had been... and celebrate her. If you're going through a similar death of identity, I invite you to do the same. Ask someone you trust to write a eulogy for the version of you that is ready to be laid to rest. Let them reflect the beauty you forgot to see. Use it as a way to honor the soul you're shedding—and the soul you're stepping into.

Because this moment, as painful as it may be, is your initiation.

Letting go isn't about failure. It's about release. It's about shedding the parts of you that no longer reflect your truth. It's about creating space to rise as the version of you who no longer waits to be chosen—but chooses yourself, fully and without apology. It's about learning to rest instead of hustle. To listen instead of push. To allow instead of proving.

This part of the journey taught me how to be with myself in the unknown. I learned to trust that not knowing is a sacred place, not a punishment. Some days, I still get lost in the wilderness of transformation. On other days, I feel completely free. But through it all, I've come to see that I am the one who chooses who I become. And when I stop gripping the past and say yes to what's next... the path opens in ways I could never have planned.

Staying present with your feelings is a key way to build trust not just in life but also in yourself. That emotional range—the ability to sit with grief, hope, resistance, joy—is what makes you whole. Your strength isn't in how fast you bounce back. It's in how deeply you're willing to sit with yourself as you become someone new.

Becoming your highest self is not about perfection—it's about wholeness. And wholeness looks different for everyone. It's not always bliss and clarity. Sometimes, it's fog and fatigue. But when you commit to knowing and loving all aspects of yourself, you build an inner foundation that can withstand anything. You become the steady presence you were always looking for.

Becoming this version of myself didn't happen overnight. It was a creative, soul-led process. However, six core concepts helped me bridge the inner gap between who I was and who I am now. In the next section, I'll share those with you... not as a formula but as a framework to help you meet yourself in the middle of your own becoming.

Bridging the Gap Between Who You've Been and Who You're Becoming

Becoming your highest self is not about rushing to a finish line. It's about crossing an invisible threshold from old patterns to a new embodiment of truth. And while the journey of transformation can feel uncertain, there are grounded, practical ways to walk yourself through it—step by step, breath by breath.

These six tools are meant to help you bridge the internal gap between the version of you that was shaped by survival... and the version of you that was born for sovereignty.

This isn't about becoming someone else. It's about finally meeting the person you were always meant to be.

1. Explore Who You're Becoming

Self-discovery is a sacred reclamation. When you begin to witness yourself without judgment, you open the doorway to your next evolution. This phase is about making contact with the version of you that's been waiting on the other side of letting go.

Start journaling what's rising within you. Track the subtle shifts in your thoughts, emotions, and longings. When you name your

Twin Flame Obsession

desires, you give them permission to breathe. When you meet your truth, you stand in your power.

Here are a few prompts to support that unfolding:

- I envision my highest self as someone who...
- My future self thinks, feels, and acts like...
- Becoming one with my sacred self means...
- I want to be my best self because...
- When I am fully me, I show up by...

Let the answers come slowly. Let them surprise you. This isn't about defining yourself in one journal entry. It's about listening to the truth you've long silenced—and honoring the path that unfolds when you finally hear it.

2. Observe Your Obstacles with Curiosity
Every block on your path is an invitation to return to yourself.

Most of the time, we assume the pain is about someone else—their actions, their silence, their inability to meet us where we are. However, the truth is that our reactions to those moments are where the real work lies. When you become the observer of your own story, patterns begin to reveal themselves. Old wounds surface. And clarity returns.

As a child, I often stayed quiet. My father was a talker, and I learned to listen—not out of interest but because it was safer to remain silent. I never fully learned how to express myself. That pattern followed me into adulthood and into my relationships. I realized one day, while watching a father and daughter walking together in the neighborhood, how much I still longed for that kind of open connection. It made me reflect on how my communication in my relationships mirrored my childhood dynamic. I was finally ready to break the pattern—not by blaming, but by listening, learning, and expressing myself more openly.

When you observe without judgment, you reclaim your power to change. And when you stop projecting your healing onto others, you begin to bridge the gap from who you've been... to who you truly are.

3. Envision Your Ideal Self

Who are you when you stop trying to prove, fix, or earn love?

Your ideal self already lives within you. But to embody them, you must first see them clearly. Visualization is a powerful tool for shifting out of survival mode and into a state of sovereignty. When you feel, think, and act in alignment with the version of you that's already whole, you begin to embody them.

Ask yourself:

- What does my ideal day look like?
- How do I speak to myself when I'm my highest self?
- What emotions do I carry when I walk through the world as my truest me?
- What habits, boundaries, and beliefs support this version of me?
- What's currently standing in the way—and is it even mine?

See yourself on the other side of your story. That future version of you already exists. They're not waiting for someone to choose them. They're waiting for *you* to choose *you*.

4. Map Your Quest with Intention

You may not control your circumstances, but you *do* control how you meet them.

You are the architect of your reality. And while you may not always know the whole picture, you can still choose the next step. That's what makes this part sacred. It's not about having it all figured out—it's about showing up to your own becoming with reverence and resolve.

Set goals that feel true to your heart—not to the pressure of others. Make lists. Create vision boards. *Start tracking where your energy wants to go. What do you desire? What brings you fulfillment? What lights you up, even on the hardest days?*

Your soul doesn't require perfection. It craves passion. Choose with clarity. Walk with intention. And honor the fact that the map doesn't need to be finished for the journey to begin.

5. Stay Present with the Process

Healing happens in the *now*.

We often try to rewrite the past or predict the future. But transformation lives in the present. The only real power you have is in this moment—how you breathe, how you show up, how you choose again.

My grandmother used to say, "Don't borrow trouble." It took me years to understand the wisdom in that. But now I know: every time I abandon the present moment, I abandon myself.

When you stay present, you reconnect to your body. You reclaim your breath. You stop spinning in stories—and start living from your center.

Presence is where peace lives.

6. Embrace the Becoming

There is no singular moment when you *arrive*. Becoming your best self is a fluid, living experience.

The world will tell you that unless you've reached some external milestone—money, relationship, success—you don't get to enjoy your life. But the truth is that the journey itself is where the magic lives. You don't need to earn joy. You don't have to prove your worth. You are allowed to rest, to celebrate, to love your process— even while you're still in the thick of it.

Allow yourself to experience the full spectrum of being human. Laugh. Grieve. Be messy. Be magnificent. You don't have to be perfect. You just have to be *present*.

Because the real destination… is *you*.

You're not waiting for life to begin. You're living it now.

And the more you embrace that, the more your life will rise to meet you—moment by moment, breath by breath, choice by sacred choice.

The Lie That This Was Your Only Shot

There's a silent fear that creeps in when you begin to loosen your grip. It doesn't always roar; sometimes, it lingers in the quietest moments of doubt. It's that flicker of panic that may be the most profound connection you'll ever feel. That no one else will ever understand your soul quite like they did. That if you walk away now, you might miss something sacred that was just on the edge of becoming real. As if letting go means giving up on the one thing that once made everything else make sense.

But that fear isn't rooted in truth—it's rooted in trauma. It's the imprint of old wounds that equate pain with significance. It's the inner child that believes intensity is proof of destiny. It's the nervous system that has learned to cling to chaos because it once felt like love. The fear tells you to hold on tighter, to wait longer, to keep believing that suffering is part of the path.

But what if that's the lie?

What if this isn't the end of love—but the beginning of a new kind of love? One that doesn't require your heartbreak to feel holy. One that doesn't leave you waiting to be chosen. One that meets you fully, without the chase.

This is the fear most people don't talk about. The one that blends spiritual devotion with emotional scarcity. The one that convinces you to keep holding on—not because they're showing up, but because you're afraid no one else ever will. So you stay. You shrink a little. You dim your light just enough to maintain the energetic tether. You convince yourself you're being loyal, patient, and sur-rendered. That it's all part of divine timing.

But beneath that devotion is a deeper wound whispering: *What if this was it? What if there's no more love waiting for me?*

And that belief keeps you stuck in spiritual loops that glorify suffering. You start calling red flags karmic lessons. You wait for breadcrumbs and call them divine signs. You mistake adrenaline for fate and inconsistency for depth.

But here's the truth you need to remember: Love is infinite. It doesn't exist in only one name, one body, or one timeline. Yes, your twin flame cracked you open—but they are not the only vessel through which love can reach you. You are the source. You are the magnet. You are the one who carries that capacity forward with or without them.

Letting go of them doesn't close the door on love. It opens the door to the kind of love that doesn't ask you to suffer to feel worthy of it. So when the fear rises—and it will—when your chest tightens and your mind races, remind yourself gently: *You're not letting go of your only chance at love. You're letting go of the belief that love only comes through pain.*

And that shift? That's where the absolute freedom begins.

The Child Who Equated Letting Go with Being Left

Letting go doesn't always begin as a conscious choice. Sometimes, it's your nervous system that resists before your mind can catch up. You say, *"I can't let go."* But what your body hears is something far older: *"We're being abandoned again."*

And just like that, you're no longer your grown, present-day self. You're the child. The one who watched someone leave and didn't understand why. The one who tried to be perfect, helpful, quiet—hoping it would be enough to make someone stay. The one who learned that love meant clinging and that staying meant survival.

So now, when surrender is what your soul needs most, your inner child panics. Letting go doesn't feel like a conscious act of healing. It feels like being left behind—again. Even if the relationship is hurting you. Even if the silence is unbearable. Even if the signs all point to release. There's a part of you still whispering, *"Don't go. Don't give up. If you wait just a little longer... maybe this time, they'll choose you."*

That's why surrender feels so heavy—so impossible at times. Because you're not just letting go of a person. You're laying to rest a version of yourself—the one who believed your worth, safety, and identity depended on being chosen. And without that external anchor, the question lingers quietly beneath it all: *Who am I now?*

That's the void. That's the grief. That's the illusion you must release.

But healing doesn't begin by shaming the part of you that still wants to hold on. It starts by sitting with them. By telling your inner child gently, *"You're not being left. This time, we're choosing something better. This time, we're choosing us."*

Because you're not the child waiting at the window anymore. You're the soul walking yourself home.

Letting Go Was Never About Losing Them

What if the most challenging part of letting go isn't about losing someone else—but about confronting the pieces of yourself that you tied to their presence?

Letting go forces you to look at everything you projected onto them: the fantasy, the future, the version of you that would finally feel enough in their love. And when they slip away, so does that version. It's not just grief—it's identity collapse. It's realizing you weren't just holding onto them. You were holding onto who you hoped to become in their eyes.

That's what makes this hurt so different. It's not just about detaching from a person. It's about detaching from the narrative you built around them—the meaning you gave their arrival, the worth you wrapped around their approval, the story you told yourself that their love would finally make it all make sense.

But letting go doesn't mean that meaning disappears. It means you now have the power to give that meaning back to yourself.

Because what they activated in you—your capacity to feel deeply, to love endlessly, to hope, to heal, to believe in something beyond logic—was never theirs to give or take away. That was always yours.

Letting go isn't a rejection of the connection; it's a natural part of it. It's an act of reverence. It says: *Thank you for waking this up in me. I'll take it from here.*

And that's where true freedom begins—not when they return, not when it all makes sense, but when you stop looking backward and start reclaiming every part of yourself you once gave away in the name of love.

Crossing the Threshold: Tools to Come Back to You

Letting go isn't a single moment of release—it's a sacred return. It's a daily devotion to the present. A conscious crossing from who you thought you had to be into the truth of who you already are. These tools aren't about erasing the past or "getting over" them. They're about helping you discover who you were meant to be. Not in bitterness. Not in resistance. But in reverence. With grace. With choice. With love.

Journal Practice: The Truth Beneath the Clinging

Settle into stillness. Light a candle if it helps you feel held. Take a few breaths to drop into your body. Let these prompts guide you into the spaces you've been too strong to feel—until now:

- What am I terrified will happen if I let go?
- Who do I believe I'll stop being if I'm no longer tied to this story?
- What feeling do I fear I'll never experience again if I let this person go?
- What parts of me have I silenced, abandoned, or hidden to keep the fantasy alive?

Write from your belly. Let the answers rise without judgment. There's gold in your honesty.

Ritual: The Surrender Ceremony

You don't have to wait for closure to find peace. Let this ritual become your turning point. One that doesn't depend on them. One that anchors you back into your own heart.

Find a quiet space. Hold something that represents the connection—a letter, a crystal, a song. Place your hands over your heart. Feel what's still living there.

When you're ready, speak these words out loud:

> *"I release the need to control what isn't mine to carry.*
> *I release the illusion that I must be chosen to be worthy.*
> *I return to my body. I return to my truth. I return to myself.*
> *I choose peace over potential.*
> *I choose presence over pain.*
> *I choose me."*

You may cry. You may tremble. You may feel an exhale you didn't know you were holding. Whatever rises, let it be medicine. You're not letting go of love. You're letting go of the version of it that cost you your wholeness.

Affirmation to Anchor the Shift

Let this mantra become your inner compass—something you return to every time the ache whispers that you're losing something sacred.

> *"I do not lose love by letting go. I make space for the kind of love that honors me."*

Say it when the longing returns. Say it when you wake. Say it when you're standing in the mirror, unsure of what's next. Say it until your nervous system softens and your heart starts to believe.

Because this space you're creating?

It isn't empty.
It's holy.
It's yours.

Letting Go Isn't the End—It's the Return

This isn't where your story ends—it's where you finally come back to yourself. The part of you who stayed through every high and low, who whispered truth beneath every illusion, who quietly knew all along that love should never cost your sanity, your power, or your sense of self. Letting go doesn't deny the connection. It simply means that the part of you that once needed it to become something specific has outgrown the need to control how it unfolds.

You've stopped outsourcing your worth to someone else's presence. You've stopped measuring your value by how much someone stays. Because now you see it clearly—the closure you needed didn't come from a conversation or a comeback. It came from finally deciding that your wholeness was never up for debate.

More importantly, letting go isn't where the love ends—it's where your power begins. It's not a loss. It's a liberation. A conscious choice to stop overextending for someone who can't meet you. To stop holding onto something simply because it once sparked hope. It's the moment you stop proving your worth and start honoring the version of you who finally knows it.

The part of you who stayed too long tried too hard, and held on too tightly—that version carried you as far as they could. But now, it's time to lay them down gently. Thank them. And step forward as the one who no longer sacrifices peace for the sake of possibility.

You've seen the cycle. You've felt the ache. You've asked all the questions that never came with answers. And in that silence, something beautiful happened: you stopped waiting for closure and created it within yourself.

Because this was never about finding "the one." It was about remembering the one thing you'd forgotten—yourself.

And now… you're not waiting anymore.

You're *rising*.

Part Three

The Shift to Self

CHAPTER 07
BREAK THE BOND, NOT THE LOVE

I can honor the love without abandoning myself.

Let's get something straight. Letting go of your twin flame doesn't mean you have to stop loving them. You don't have to delete every photo, block every memory, or pretend you never felt the depth of the connection. You're not required to shut down your heart or become someone you're not just to survive the silence.

However, what you can't do is abandon yourself to keep the connection alive.

At some point, the cost becomes too high. Leaking your life force into something that no longer nourishes your soul isn't loyalty—it's self-neglect. And calling obsession "alignment" or heartbreak "awakening" only delays the healing your spirit is begging for.

You can honor the connection without staying bound to the pain. You can hold the love without staying stuck in the loop. And you can let go of the energetic grip without closing your heart.

This isn't about forgetting them. It's about releasing the emotional contract that says your peace depends on their return. It's about detaching from the belief that closure can only come through them. It's about calling your energy back from all the places it's been trapped—memories, timelines, conversations, unspoken hopes—and bringing it back to you.

You're not here to erase the past. You're here to end the cycle that keeps you repeating it. Because underneath the pain is a version of you who remembers your worth. One who knows love doesn't require waiting to be real. One who can feel deeply without losing themselves in fantasy. One who no longer trades their wholeness for a connection that won't stand in its fullness.

In this chapter, we'll explore the truth about energetic cords—what they are, how they form, and why releasing them isn't betrayal. It's liberation. We'll look at why neutrality is your superpower, how detachment is an act of self-love, and what it really takes to reclaim your energy from someone who's no longer showing up for you.

Because you don't need to stop loving them.

You just need to stop losing yourself in the name of that love.

Cutting the Cord Without Losing Yourself

I discovered it wasn't just one cord I had to cut—it was a lifetime of them. Threads stretched across dimensions, past lives, and multiple versions of myself. Some connections were deeply entangled, feeling almost impossible to escape, while others lingered quietly in the background or disappeared without warning. Each one mirrored something in me—my pain, my power, my purpose—and each left an imprint. For years, I called those imprints love.

I convinced myself it was divine timing. I interpreted every synchronicity as a reason to stay energetically open. I let the pull become the proof, and I built energetic altars for each of them—whether through thought, memory, emotion, or vibration. Even when the contact ended, the connection continued. They showed up like ghosts in my dreams, in music, in sudden waves of sensation that flushed through my body and left me motionless. Sometimes, I'd feel them thinking of me. Other times, I'd hear them during meditation or sense their name seconds before it appeared on my screen.

A part of me held onto the connection because it felt sacred. It felt safe. It gave my pain a story, a shape, a kind of purpose. But eventually, I began to feel the cost of that purpose in my body. The fatigue. The fragmentation. The subtle but constant sense that I wasn't fully here. That I was always partway elsewhere—part in my body and part entangled in energies I hadn't released.

Eventually, I realized I wasn't in a relationship. I was in an energetic leak.

That realization didn't strike all at once. It built over time—through quiet disappointments, repeated patterns, and the slow drain I kept trying to ignore. It wasn't about erasing the love. It was about facing the truth: I was pouring energy into something that no longer fed my soul.

There was no sage, no sound bowls, no full moon. No altar or playlist playing in the background. Just me—raw, alone, and finally done. I am not done loving, but I am done leaking.

I had been carrying them for too long. Holding space in my thoughts. Checking in through energy. Feeling them in the silence. It crept in quietly, one memory at a time, one emotional pull after another, until I could no longer deny it. I wasn't being held in return. I was the only one still in it. And I had to choose to stop bleeding energy into something that wasn't choosing me back.

And I couldn't fix it with logic. I couldn't think my way through it. I had to feel it. All of it. The grief, the hope, the fantasy I had been silently keeping alive. I sat on the floor, back against the wall, hand on my chest. No script. No performance. Just truth.

And I spoke it out loud—not to Spirit, not to them, but to myself. "I release the attachment. I honor the love. But I call my energy home."

And I meant it.

It wasn't a magic spell. But I felt it. A shift. A subtle, almost imperceptible return. Like little pieces of me unclenching. Like something heavy lifting off my back. Like strength I hadn't felt in months, beginning to stir in my belly.

That's how I knew something had changed. Not because they reached out. Not because the signs stopped. But because I didn't need them to. I could feel myself coming back.

Not to who I was before—but to who I became because of it all.

And that was enough.

It Wasn't Love That Hurt—It Was Attachment

This is where most of us get confused. We assume the pain we're feeling is because of love. We mistake the ache, the anxiety, and the tension that coils in our chest as proof that the connection must be real. And the more it hurts, the more we convince ourselves it's meant to be. But real love doesn't create suffering—attachment does.

Love is expansive. It opens us. It breathes life into us. It liberates and blesses. Attachment, on the other hand, contracts. It clings. It fears. It tries to control. Love whispers, "I want you to be free," while attachment demands, "I need you to make me feel safe."

In twin-flame dynamics, the line between the two becomes dangerously blurry. When someone activates a part of your soul you never knew existed, it's easy to confuse that activation with obligation. When someone reflects a truth, a gift, or a wound you've never fully claimed, it's tempting to believe they're the only one who can carry it with you. But the connection was never meant to become a cage.

You can honor the soul bond without becoming enslaved by it. You can love someone with your whole heart and still walk away from what's draining your energy. You can appreciate the role they played in your awakening and still choose your peace. The intensity you feel isn't always a sign of destiny—it's often a reflection of unhealed dependency. Sometimes, what you think is divine alignment is actually trauma responding, not truth.

What we're rarely taught is this: you don't have to sever the soul connection to heal. You just have to cut the cords—the energetic threads that keep you spiraling in obsessive thought, the pull that leaves you ungrounded, the way your body tenses when their name enters your field, the way your joy dims without explanation. These are the cords. That's the bondage. And that's what you have permission to release—without guilt, without shame, and without losing the love.

Because the love was real. But the suffering? That part is optional.

The Invisible Threads That Keep You Bound

Before you can release the cords, you have to name them. The anxiety that creeps in when you sense their energy. The mental looping that takes over your thoughts. The sudden wave of exhaustion that hits the moment they cross your mind. The ache that lingers—not tied to one memory but woven through your entire system. This isn't just emotion. It's energy. And it's trying to get your attention.

These threads may not always be visible, but they are deeply felt. They're formed not just by love or intimacy but by trauma, unmet needs, and unspoken expectations. They attach in moments of vulnerability, spark during emotional highs, and embed themselves through repetition. Over time, they wrap around your energy like vines—some gently, others with a grip so tight it's hard to breathe. What started as a connection slowly transformed into entanglement. The thread doesn't just link you to them—it slowly pulls you out of alignment with yourself.

A healthy cord feels like a mutual connection. It supports you. It respects your evolution. It uplifts you while honoring both people's freedom. But unhealthy cords? They grip. They drain. They feed on longing and keep you chasing a feeling you haven't truly experienced in a long time.

You'll recognize unhealthy cords by the way they manifest. Emotional obsession. Anxiety when they go quiet. Panic at the thought of letting go. The belief that you're incomplete without them. The need for signs, readings, or rituals just to feel close again. That's not a soul bond—that's entanglement.

You're not just remembering them. You're still energetically tied to them—not through love, but through unresolved energy, not through presence, but through depletion. The cord is what keeps the loop alive. And unless you consciously release it, you'll continue to leak energy into a connection that no longer gives back.

This isn't about denying the love. It's about disentangling from the parts of the bond that are keeping you stuck. You're not breaking the love—you're breaking the bondage. And once you do that, you create space for something sacred. The kind of love that doesn't require suffering to prove its depth.

When Thinking of Them No Longer Hurts

Let's be honest—there was a time when even the thought of them could unground you. Not just from a post or a dream, but by way of a particular smell in the air, the rhythm of a phrase, or the sound of someone's voice in a crowded room could jolt your heart. *Why does it hit you so hard?* Because the remembrance is cellular. A flicker of their essence embedded in everyday life that could knock you sideways when you least expected it.

Therefore, the pain goes way beyond missing them. It's about the way their energy still lingers in your body like a phantom signal. The reflex to search for their presence. The familiar pull to decode the silence. You weren't simply triggered by the past—you were responding to a pattern still imprinted in your system, one that hadn't been fully released.

But healing rewrites that experience.

Healing is when you can think of them and stay regulated. When your breath remains steady, and your center holds. When a memory no longer pulls you under, and the thought of them doesn't take over your day. That is neutrality. Not the kind that comes from shutting down or going numb—but the kind that arises from integration. It doesn't mean you stopped caring. It means you're no longer consumed.

Neutrality isn't detachment out of defense—it's presence without pain. It's remembrance without reattachment. It's the shift where they no longer define your worth or determine your mood. And this state of being? This is the place your soul has been trying to reach all along. Because neutrality is power. It doesn't mean the connection wasn't real—it means you are real. And you no longer need to bleed for love to prove it.

When you reach this place, it's not that you've stopped feeling. It's that you've started choosing yourself—again and again, no matter who shows up or who doesn't. That kind of peace is unshakable. And it's not the end of your love story. It's the beginning of a new era where you finally become the center of your own energy.

Releasing the Tie Without Closing Your Heart

Cutting the cord doesn't mean cutting someone out of your heart. It means releasing the grip they have on your energy. Somewhere along the way, "holding space" became a form of self-abandonment. "Staying open" morphed into emotional depletion. And your love—pure, potent, infinite—became entangled in a pattern of waiting, hoping, and clinging to something that was no longer nourishing your soul.

Freedom doesn't require erasure. You don't need to block them out of spite or delete every message to reclaim your strength. You can choose something deeper. Something truer. Energetic sovereignty. It's the conscious act of reclaiming your field, re-centering your frequency, and protecting your peace—not out of bitterness, but because you're done leaking your life force into something that no longer reciprocates.

That's the truth about cord-cutting. It's not about closing your heart—it's about containing your power. Sometimes, that might look like unfollowing them—not as punishment, but because every scroll scrapes at your nervous system. It may mean stepping away from rituals, readings, or channeling that keep you tethered in ways that no longer serve you. It might mean saying no to communication, even if they reach out because your energy is still stabilizing and sacred.

But the most essential truth? You don't have to stop loving them. You just have to stop abandoning yourself in the name of that love. Because real love doesn't ask you to sacrifice yourself at the altar of someone else's evolution. Real love makes space for you to return to your own.

You can still honor what the connection awakened in you—without staying trapped in its absence. You can let go without shutting down. You can release the bond without rejecting the beauty it once held. And when you cut the cord with love, what you're really saying is:

> *"I carry the love, but I no longer carry the weight.*
> *I keep the lesson, but I let go of the loop.*
> *I choose peace.*
> *I choose presence.*
> *I choose me."*

Energetic Grieving: Letting Go of the Future That Never Came

Letting go isn't just about releasing what happened—it's about mourning what never did. One of the most painful aspects of this journey is the silent grief of unlived timelines. The vision you held. The life you imagined. The conversations you were certain would happen someday. The reunion you rehearsed in your mind more times than you could count.

And when those imagined futures begin to fade, it can feel like losing them all over again.

But what you're feeling isn't just about missing them—it's about releasing everything you built around them. The imagined future. The meanings you assign to every interaction. The way you molded your timeline around their potential. You're mourning the story you told yourself while trying to make sense of the connection. Not because you were foolish but because you were faithful. You wanted to believe it all had a divine purpose. That the pain was part of a greater plan. That one day, it would all come full circle. Letting go now isn't just about surrendering the bond—it's about unweaving the narrative that kept you waiting for a love that never learned how to stay.

This grief can be complicated to name because it doesn't always take a specific form. There are no photos to burn or messages to reread. Only thoughts. Longings. Timelines that never took root.

But the grief is real. And it deserves space.

Energetic grieving means honoring the loss without shaming yourself for feeling it. It's allowing the tears for what never came to pass. It's placing your hand on your heart and saying, "I release the future I planned around you. I release the version of us that only existed in my hope."

This doesn't mean you failed. It means you're waking up from the trance. And in that awakening, you make room for a new vision—one that includes your peace, your wholeness, and your power at the center.

If you feel the need to mourn, let yourself. Light a candle. Write a letter to the timeline that never happened. Say goodbye to the version of you who stayed waiting. The version of you that was brave. They believed in love. But now it's your turn to believe in yourself.

And as you grieve, know this: you're not closing the door on love. You're closing the door on depletion. What's meant for you won't require you to wait in pain for it to arrive. What's real will meet you here—in this timeline, in this breath, in the wholeness of who you are now.

The Sacred Return: Tools to Call Your Energy Home

This journey isn't just about letting go—it's about calling yourself back. Because every thought, every spiral, every sleepless night spent swimming in memories has cost you something. The constant energetic reaching, the analyzing, the channeling, the what-ifs... all of it chipped away at your center. And now, it's time to reclaim what's yours.

These tools aren't about forgetting the connection. They're not about erasing the soul bond or pretending it didn't matter. They're here to help you release the weight of carrying it alone. You don't need to cut the soul—only the cords that have pulled you out of alignment. This is about resetting your system. Clearing the noise. Anchoring your power. And remembering that your energy is sacred. It deserves to live inside of you.

Journal Practice: Untangling the Threads

Use these prompts to drop beneath the surface and write with complete honesty. Let your truth come through—not the spiritualized version or the story you've been telling yourself to stay hopeful. This is for the part of you that's ready to be real, raw, and rooted.

- What part of me still feels entangled with them?
- What am I afraid will happen if I release this energy?
- What does my body feel when I imagine being entirely disconnected?
- How can I love them… without leaving myself behind?

Let your answers guide you into clarity—not just mentally, but energetically.

Cord-Cutting Ritual: The Homecoming Ceremony

This isn't about force. It's about reverence.

Begin by sitting in stillness. Hold something that symbolizes the connection—a photo, a crystal, a letter, anything tangible that holds meaning. Place one hand over your heart and the other on your lower belly. Close your eyes and visualize every thread of energy you've sent out to this person—through hope, through longing, through pain—beginning to return.

Breathe slowly and intentionally. With each inhale, whisper:

"I call my power back from everyone, and everywhere I've left it. I am whole. I am home."

As you exhale, imagine the energetic residue dissolving—leaving your field like smoke rising and disappearing into the air. Let yourself feel the release. Let it be soft. Let it be sacred.

Repeat this as often as you need. This is how your body learns what it means to be sovereign again. It's not a one-time event. It's a reclamation. A homecoming.

Affirmation to Anchor Your Energy

Let this affirmation be the anchor you reach for anytime your energy starts to scatter or your heart starts to drift toward the loop:

> *"I break the bond—not the love.*
> *I release the pain—not the lesson.*
> *I reclaim my peace.*
> *And I return to me."*

Say it when you wake up. Say it when the pull creeps in. Say it until your body believes you.

Because this isn't just healing. This is your sacred return.

The Bond Was Never the Love—You Were

You were never meant to carry it forever—not the weight of the memories, not the ache of what might have been, and indeed not the looping thoughts that kept you energetically tethered to someone who left you open, waiting, and emotionally shattered. You weren't here to abandon yourself in search of connection or confuse emotional burnout with proof of love. This was never about calling spiritual exhaustion a soul connection or using your suffering as proof that it was sacred.

The bond itself wasn't what made it holy. You did. You were the sacred thread. The way you loved. The way you stayed soft, even when it hurt. The way you kept showing up for something invisible because your heart told you it was real. And it was real. However, it was never meant to compromise your clarity. It was never meant to drain your joy or fragment your sovereignty in the name of staying "open."

You don't have to forget them to be free. You don't have to erase the signs or rewrite the past. You can still honor the connection and choose to release the version of it that left you divided. Letting go doesn't mean the love disappears—it means the love gets to evolve. It gets to include you now. It becomes something that doesn't leave you spiraling or waiting or split between timelines. It becomes something grounded, embodied, and whole.

Letting go isn't about becoming hard or detached; it's about embracing a new perspective. This is about becoming complete. It's about calling your spirit back from every place you left it—in memories, in moments, in future fantasies that never arrived. It's about realizing that the most sacred union was never meant to be found in someone else.

It's the one where your love and your power live in the same place.

Inside you.

CHAPTER 08
FROM CHASER TO CREATOR

I'm done chasing—it's time to choose me.

You were never meant to chase. You were born to create.

But when you're caught in chaser energy, it rarely feels like chasing. It feels like holding on, like trusting the journey, like doing the work. You convince yourself that staying loyal to the connection is part of your spiritual purpose. You interpret the ache as something sacred. You mistake obsession for proof of unconditional love.

But if we're being honest, the longer you chase, the more disconnected you become from yourself. The more your energy is directed outward—toward them, their healing, their timing—the more depleted you feel. You may call it devotion, but your body knows the truth. It's not devotion—it's a drain.

Every thought. Every ritual. Every moment you spend monitoring, manifesting, or managing the outcome is energy leaving your field. The energy that could be nourishing your body. Fueling your next breakthrough. Calling you deeper into your brilliance and your becoming.

This chapter isn't about becoming cold or shutting down. It's about becoming whole. Whole enough to stop grasping for love outside yourself. Whole enough to stop trying to prove your worth through someone else's attention. Whole enough to recognize that the energy you've been pouring out wasn't wasted—it was simply misplaced.

Now, it's time to recalibrate.

It's time to retire the identity of the chaser and reclaim your power. To break the cycle of energetic self-sacrifice. To recognize the patterns that have been draining your vitality and redirect that energy into something sacred—something creative, nourishing, and self-honoring. To shift your focus toward joy, clarity, and the kind of self-connection that creates lasting peace from within.

Because healing isn't just about letting go. It's about re-creation. And every ounce of love you've been giving away? It was always meant to build something bigger. It was always meant to bring you back to you.

The Mirror That Made Me Write This Book

This wasn't my first collision. Not by a long shot. I had met reflections of myself many times before—each one holding a piece of my becoming. Each one arriving to help me reclaim another part of my truth.

But this one was different.

It was a bright morning in Panama City Beach. I was walking into my condo complex as he was walking out. We passed each other in the lobby, and I casually said, "It's a beautiful day out there." He stopped. Turned around. Looked straight at me and asked, "What did you just say?"

I repeated it. He smiled slowly and said, "Your accent." He was from another country, so to him, *I* was the one with the accent.

But it wasn't about the words. Something in the air had shifted. The world didn't just slow down—it stopped. Fifteen minutes felt like fifteen days. Our first date lasted seven hours, but it felt like seven months. Every moment, every word, every breath between us

134

carried a sense of déjà vu, as if they had existed long before we ever spoke them aloud.

And then came the names. When I told him mine—Harmony—and he told me his, it hit like thunder. The names didn't just sound good together; they also had a certain charm. They felt like a frequency. Like rhythm and melody. As if the Universe had orchestrated the whole thing. Just then, the office manager walked in while we were still talking. I introduced him, and when she heard our names side by side, she looked at us and said, "Well, if that isn't a match made in heaven."

I laughed, but something inside me stirred.

He was an author. Wise beyond his years. Thirty-two—twenty-six years younger than me. Younger than my own children. And yet, he was more emotionally present than most men I had ever known. He saw me. He spoke to me with reverence. He called me a goddess— not because I asked him to, but because I was. We discussed life, legacy, writing, and soul purpose. He asked me to be his life partner. He opened his heart without hesitation. He felt my walls and asked me to let them down.

And for the first time in my life, I felt what it meant to be fully met.

But I couldn't receive it.
Not like that.
Not in that package.
Not in that moment.

I became the runner—not because he wasn't enough, but because his presence made me question everything I thought I had already healed. So I ended it. I told myself I was being practical. That it couldn't work. That it was too complicated, too much, too fast.

But afterward, I spiraled—deeper than I had in years.

Because when I ended it, it crushed him. And I could feel his pain so deeply it cracked me open even more. It was visceral. His grief lived in my body like it was my own. And the more open I became, the more I felt our connection stretch beyond logic—like it was still alive, pulsing in the space between us.

We stayed connected quietly, delicately. During that time, a few things happened in his life that brought him to his own edge—things that reflected back his fear of being a burden. He didn't want to weigh me down with what he was carrying. So I honored that. I gave him space. Not as an excuse to run but as an act of love. A way to let him heal without the pressure of maintaining the relationship.

Still, he didn't just mirror my wounds. He mirrored my work. My worth. My womanhood. My becoming. He showed me the goddess I had fought to embody. He reflected the radiance I had cultivated in silence. And that's what made the letting go even harder. Because for the first time, it wasn't just about releasing someone who hurt me. It was about releasing someone who saw me—and who I saw just as clearly.

And walking alone on the beach, I realized something: this wasn't about him coming back. It was about me coming home.

I asked myself, "What do I want now?" Not from him. Not from the ache. Not from the past. From me. That question rewired everything.

I didn't chase. I didn't perform spiritual devotion. I didn't try to manifest him back. Instead, I created. I poured my energy into this book. My mission. I anchored into my joy. I honored the connection without collapsing into it.

Because he wasn't my ending—he was the threshold.

That's when I realized I don't have to orchestrate love. I only have to embody the frequency of what I'm ready to receive. He reminded me that I am magnetic. That I am whole. That I don't have to chase what's already aligned.

And from that moment on, I stopped waiting.

I started creating.

Retiring the Role That Was Never Yours

The chasers don't chase because they're desperate. They chase because, somewhere along the line, they were taught that love had to be earned. That devotion meant endurance. That silence was a test of worthiness. That if someone pulled away, it was their responsibility to close the gap. And so, they learned to give. To wait. To prove. To hold on—no matter the cost. Not because they were weak but because they were wired that way.

If you grew up in a home where love was conditional, where affection was given based on behavior, where your emotions weren't mirrored, or where your needs weren't consistently met, then chasing may have become your default language of love. It's not that you wanted to beg for connection—it's that you didn't believe you could simply receive it. So you became the over-giver. The one who stayed. The one who waited. The one who bent, overextended, sacrificed, and surrendered to the point of self-erasure, believing that if you just held on long enough, they would come around.

You may have called it unconditional love. But beneath it lived a quiet, unspoken truth: fear. Fear of being abandoned. Fear of being forgotten. Fear of not being chosen—again.

But you were never meant to chase love. You were meant to embody it.

The chaser is not your identity—it's your adaptation. A survival strategy built from early wounds. A role you stepped into to make sense of pain. A mask you wore to feel in control. And now? You get to take it off. You get to retire the role—not with shame, but with sovereignty. Because chasing was never who you were.

You are not here to prove your worth through someone else's awakening. You are not here to earn love through suffering. You are not here to wait on someone else's timeline to validate your own. You are here to create alignment. To claim your energy. To remember that the version of you who chased was never wrong—just exhausted.

And now, that version is ready to rise.

Your Power Was Never Gone—It Was Just Misplaced

Let's discuss where your energy has been directed.

Every time you replay that conversation in your mind... every time you check their social media hoping for a sign... every time you light a candle, pull a card, or beg the Universe for a breakthrough—you're spending energy. The energy that could be nourishing your body. Fueling your creativity. Anchoring you deeper into your mission.

But instead, that energy is leaking into an outcome you can't control. And it's not just spiritual energy. It's emotional. Mental. Even physical. How many nights have you struggled to sleep because your thoughts were wrapped around them? How many mornings have you delayed your purpose, waiting to "feel better" first? How many days have passed where your joy, your clarity, and your creativity were paused—because your soul was still tethered to someone else's timeline?

Let's call this what it is: you've been outsourcing your power. Not because you're broken. Not because you don't know better. But because love felt safer when it had a target. Because longing gave your feelings somewhere to land. Because obsession creates a sense of control in the absence of connection. Because waiting gave you a sense of purpose when everything else felt uncertain.

But none of those things are serving your expansion. In fact, they've been stalling it.

Here's a reality check: you're not out of energy. You've just been investing it in the wrong direction. And the solution isn't to harden. It's not to build walls or spiritualize your shutdown with declarations of "I'm done" while still checking your phone every hour. The solution is to reclaim it—with presence, with softness, and with radical intention.

Close your eyes. Breathe deeply. Tune into all the places you've scattered your energy—past moments, future fantasies, unspoken conversations, texts that never came. And now, call it back. Feel it filling your system. Restoring your field. Powering your presence.

Because when your energy returns to you, something miraculous happens: your magnetism comes back online. You start creating again. Moving again. Glowing again—not because they returned, but because you did.

That's when everything begins to shift. Not because you finally got what you wanted. But because you finally remembered who you were.

The Quiet Ways You Give Yourself Away

Most people think power loss happens in a dramatic moment—a breakup, a betrayal, a painful goodbye. But more often? It happens quietly. In the in-between spaces. In the micro-choices. In the thoughts you've rehearsed so often, you've stopped questioning them.

You lose power every time you re-read an old message, looking for hidden meaning. Every time your stomach drops because they posted a story but didn't reach out. Every time you pull an oracle card or check astrology, hoping it will confirm that they're thinking about you. You lose power every time you wait to book the trip, start the project, or open your heart to someone new—just in case they come back.

These moments may seem small. But they accumulate. And over time, they tether you to a frequency of waiting, wondering, and withholding your own life force.

This is what I call power leakage.

It doesn't always register as pain. Sometimes, it feels like purpose. Like staying open is strength. Like the intensity is proof that it means something. You convince yourself that waiting is a form of growth. That staying connected is spiritual. That holding space is love. But what you're really doing is rehearsing heartbreak and calling it sacred. Your nervous system has mistaken the ache for alignment and the familiar pull for destiny. It's not expansion—it's entrapment dressed in devotion. And until you name it for what it is, you'll keep circling the same cycle, thinking you're ascending when, really—you're just avoiding the end.

Here's what most don't realize: you're not holding space—you're holding yourself hostage. You're delaying your joy, postponing your peace, and putting your life on hold while waiting for someone else to finally say, "I'm ready." That's not love. That's self-abandonment masked as commitment.

So, how do you stop the cycle? You begin with awareness. You start paying attention to the exact moments your power begins to leak. That quick hit of dopamine when you check their feed. The spike of anxiety when their name flashes through your mind, but your phone stays silent. The subtle hesitation to say yes to something new—just in case they reappear and throw you off course again.

Instead of defaulting to autopilot, you pause. You place your hand over your heart and ask, "Is this feeding my energy or draining it?" And then, you choose again. You take a breath. You write something honest. You move your body. You speak a boundary. You remind yourself who you are and what matters now. You anchor back into what's real—your breath, your body, your moment, your life.

Because every time you choose presence over pattern, you reclaim a thread of your power. And as those threads come together, they begin to weave a new reality—one where love doesn't require self-erasure. One where commitment feels reciprocal, not one-sided. One where your future is no longer held hostage by someone else's absence.

You are here now. Rooted. Ready. Whole.

And that is more than enough to begin again.

When You Return to You—What Comes Next?

You've called your energy back. You've cut the cords. You've stopped waiting. And now you're here—in the stillness that follows. For many, this is the most terrifying part. Because when you've spent so long chasing someone else's presence, standing fully in your own can feel unfamiliar, even empty. You catch yourself wondering, *What do I do with all this space? Where does all this energy go now?*

The answer is simple but profound: you create with it, not as a performance. Not to prove your growth. Not to secretly lure them back. But because your soul has been starving for a place to land. Creation is the return. It's how your spirit re-inhabits your body. It's how your power reclaims form. It's the bridge between longing and living.

And it doesn't have to be some big, public declaration. You don't have to launch a business or write a book—unless you want to. Sometimes, the most revolutionary thing you can do is create a new relationship with yourself. Start small. Instead of texting them, write a letter to your future self. Tell them what you've learned. What you've healed. What you're proud of. Let your own voice become the one that wraps around you like a prayer.

Instead of scrolling for signs, make a vision board for the life that lights you up. Ask yourself what joy looks like now. What colors, images, or energies reflect who you're becoming—not who you were while waiting.

Instead of pulling cards about them, build a morning ritual that belongs only to you. Light a candle. Place your hand on your heart. Ask yourself, *What does my energy need today?* And instead of waiting for a sign... become the sign. Show the Universe who you are now. Let your frequency speak louder than your fear.

This is how your life begins to shift, not all at once but with consistent, sacred acts of self-return. Dance to one song every morning in your living room. Make your coffee with gratitude, not grief. Set a nightly alarm and ask yourself, *Did I feed my energy today?* Take a walk without your phone and actually feel the air on your skin, the sun on your face, the aliveness in your breath.

These small, repeated choices aren't just habits; they're also a form of self-control. They're declarations: *I am worth my own energy.*

Creation won't erase the pain, but it will alchemize it. It transforms ache into art, obsession into embodiment, spiraling into stability. And the more you show up for yourself, the less you need to be rescued from the void—because you've filled it with your own presence.

Eventually, you won't need signs to remind you that you're okay. Your rituals will become your reminders. Your life will become your message. And your energy will become magnetic.

Tools to Turn Longing Into Legacy

You've spent so long pouring your love, your energy, and your vision into someone else. Now, it's time to pour it back into you.

Because everything you felt was real. The intensity. The passion. The ache. None of it was wasted. It was fuel. And now, it's ready to become something more.

This is the moment where longing becomes legacy. Where emotional energy transforms into spiritual embodiment. Where you stop surviving the story and begin rewriting it.

And to do that—you need tools. Practices that redirect your power with intention. Moments that help you remember who you are and what you're here to create.

Start by asking yourself the questions that bring your energy into the present. Don't censor. Don't spiritualize. Just write it raw and let the truth pour through:

- Where has my energy been going—and what has it been costing me?
- What lights me up when I'm not thinking about them?
- What desires, dreams, or projects have I been putting on hold?
- What's one thing I can create this week that reflects the truth of who I'm becoming?

These journal prompts aren't just reflections. They are reclamation. They're the doorway back to your creative current.

And once you feel that spark? Anchor it.

Begin each day with a ritual—not to prove your worth, but to direct your energy where it belongs: within.
Light a candle.
Place one hand on your heart and the other on your solar plexus.
Close your eyes and speak out loud:

> *"I direct my energy toward joy, purpose, and expansion.*
> *I create from love, not lack.*
> *I call my spirit into this day—and I trust what it wants to build through me."*

Then, do one small thing to embody that intention.
Write one page. Move your body. Speak your truth. Dance in your kitchen. Make art that no one else sees but you.
It doesn't have to be polished. It just has to be real.
Let it be messy. Let it be sacred. Let it be yours.

And when your energy starts to waver, when you forget your own frequency, return to this:

> *"I no longer chase what I already am.*
> *I create the life that calls me home."*

Write it on your mirror. Whisper it into your tea. Repeat it until your cells remember.

Because you're not waiting for alignment anymore.

You are it.

You Were Never the Chaser—You Were the Creator All Along

You thought the love was the reward—the reunion, the recognition, the return. But it never was. The real reward was who you became in the process of remembering yourself.

You've walked through longing. You've stood in the ache. You've lost yourself a hundred times just to find one message, one sign, one reason to hold on. But now? You're done holding on. Because your hands are open—for something new. Not just a person but a purpose. A path. A power that lives in your body and moves through your breath. A truth you can actually feel in your bones because it's yours.

You were never meant to stay in the waiting room for someone else's potential. You were meant to create. Bring your gifts into form. To give your energy a place to live that builds you. To turn your sacred ache into aligned action. To become the living, breathing embodiment of the love you've been holding space for.

Yes, they may have activated your light. But you are the one who carries it forward.

And now? You're not waiting. You're not spiraling. You're not shrinking yourself to fit inside the timelines that used to hurt you. You're creating. Not from lack, but from soul. Not from hope but from wholeness. Not from proving but from truth.

You're no longer the version of yourself who chases love. You're the one who chooses it. Embodies it. Becomes it.

This is your next chapter. And it's not written in obsession or longing. It's written in embodiment, in intention, in full creative power.

And this time—you hold the pen.

CHAPTER 09
HEALING THE MIRROR WITHIN

They weren't rejecting me—they were reflecting me.

Y ou keep asking the same questions: Why won't they choose me? Why do they pull away the moment I open my heart? Why do I always end up feeling like I'm being abandoned? It feels personal. Painful. Like a pattern, you can't escape no matter how much work you do. The person who pulls away isn't just creating distance. They are reflecting the places inside you where being seen feels too vulnerable. Places where exposure feels unsafe and true connection feels like a threat rather than a comfort.

It may not be rejection. It might be a revelation. An invitation to meet the parts of yourself you've long exiled. The ones who stay quiet to avoid conflict, who overextend to feel valuable, who shape-shift to be accepted. The tender inner self was taught that love had limits and that being fully seen came with a cost.

This isn't just a romance. It's a reunion. And not between two people—but between the fractured parts of you still waiting to come back home. Because every time they ghost, avoid, or shut down, they are mirroring something inside of you that's already been missing. Their silence reflects your silence with yourself. Their distance mirrors the emotional disconnect you've become accustomed to.

Their inconsistency amplifies the parts of you that have been walking on eggshells since childhood.

This is not a love story. It's a mirror. And the reflection isn't here to wound you—it's here to wake you up. You're not here to fix them. You're here to face yourself. To stop leaving behind the child who never felt emotionally safe. To hold the version of you who was told to tone it down, stay quiet, be easy, be less. The one who learned that love was earned through suppression, not self-expression. You're here to stop waiting for someone else to fill the void you've been avoiding—and to start offering yourself the presence you've always needed.

This chapter isn't about getting them back. It's about getting yourself back. It's about choosing to stay when you want to run. To feel instead of numb. To become the one who doesn't just crave love—but creates safety, sets boundaries, and honors truth from the inside out.

Because your worth was never up for negotiation, and love was never meant to be the proof. The healing begins when you stop reaching outward for validation and start reclaiming the part of you that never needed to be earned.

When Wholeness Meant Getting Naked—in Every Way

There was a time when vulnerability terrified me—not because I didn't feel, but because I had spent years mastering the art of not being seen. I thought I had done the work. And in many ways, I had. I had cracked open my heart in past relationships. I had sat in ceremonies, wept under the moon, screamed into the vortexes, and written page after page of raw revelations. I had leaned on my masculine energy to guide me with structure, logic, protection, and discipline. I had done the work—but I hadn't yet *embodied* it.

Because even though I could feel love, I couldn't always let it in. I couldn't fully immerse myself in it. I couldn't completely allow myself to be seen *inside* it.

The first time I experienced divine love, I was still navigating life through my masculine energy—leading, managing, orchestrating, protecting. I was emotionally aware, yes. I could speak vulnerability, channel it, teach it. But I wasn't living it in my body. Not yet. Not until everything started to crack.

Heartbreak after heartbreak began to strip away everything I had built around myself for safety. I felt layers falling off—old identities, protective roles, conditioned beliefs—until I stood raw, exposed, and unguarded. And though terrifying, it was also deeply beautiful. What I had believed to be a spiritual evolution was, in truth, a return to my own humanity.

I had to release the image I had clung to for so long—the strong one, the spiritual one, the together one. And underneath all of that, I met the part of me that had been waiting patiently all along: my wild, untamed, unfiltered feminine energy. She wasn't there to take over or dominate. She was simply ready to be felt. To be heard. To be held.

And for her to emerge, the masculine within me—my inner protector—had to surrender control. I could no longer orchestrate my healing. I had to become it.

Everything came to a head during a conversation with a man I deeply trusted—someone who had witnessed my evolution. But before that conversation, I found myself in the shower, trembling with tears running down my face. Not because I feared him. But because I feared being *seen*. Not just emotionally. But physically.

It hit me: I wasn't afraid of him seeing my body. I was terrified of seeing it. Scared to look at myself and say, "This is who I am—and I still deserve love."

When we talked, I told him the truth. I needed to be seen completely. I didn't need to perform or perfect. I didn't want to be held because I was strong. I wanted to be held because I was whole—even in my softness, even in my tenderness. I let myself strip down, body and soul. And he received me. With presence. With reverence. With no agenda but to hold space.

It changed something deep within me.

But the real transformation came later—on a hike through nature with a soul sister and client who was walking her own path of union within. Together, without planning it, we came upon a pool of water nestled in a crescent-shaped cave, symbolizing the womb. The void. The sacred space of rebirth.

We looked at each other—eyes wide, hearts knowing—and we stripped down naked. We stepped into that freezing water. Rubbed mud over our skin. Rinsed ourselves clean. Body. Soul. Story. It wasn't just a plunge. It was a baptism into our wholeness.

That day, I felt more liberated than I ever had in my life. Not because I had healed everything but because I had finally come home—to my breath, to my body, to my balanced self. The masculine within me no longer needed to hide behind structure or spiritual performance. The feminine no longer needed to fake softness to feel safe.

They had found each other in me. And from that inner union, I no longer feared being seen. Because I wasn't just talking about sacred love anymore. I had become it.

Becoming the One Who Stays

There was a time in my life when the person I believed to be my twin flame was the missing piece of the puzzle. He activated me. He cracked me open. He made me feel alive in a way nothing else ever had. He was the catalyst that activated my spiritual gifts to the nth degree. But what I didn't realize back then was just how fragmented I still was. I had done the work. I had walked the desert of detachment. I had rewritten every limiting belief I could find. And yet—deep down—there was a part of me still quietly waiting for someone else to arrive and hold it all together.

Over and over, I kept attracting emotionally unavailable partners. Men who would show up fully, intensely, until the moment I let my guard down. The moment I opened my heart, they would start to pull away. Go silent. Disappeared into their own confusion while I spiraled into mine. I used to think I just hadn't met the right one yet. But the more I slowed down and truly listened, especially during the moments I felt abandoned, the more I began to see the truth: I wasn't being left. I was being shown where I had been leaving myself.

Every time I second-guessed my needs… every time I silenced my truth to avoid conflict… every time I waited for a man to choose me so I could finally feel worthy… I was abandoning the one person who had been there all along: me.

I remember standing in Sedona, surrounded by the red rocks and the hum of the earth, asking the question I had asked a hundred times before: *"Why do I keep ending up in the same pattern?"* And the answer that rose up wasn't soft. It was sharp, clear, and impossible to ignore: *"Because you don't trust your own inner masculine."*

That landed like lightning.

Because it was true. I didn't fully trust myself to stay present when things got hard. I didn't trust myself to take action on my truth. I didn't trust myself to lead with love without losing myself in the process. I had devoted so much of my energy to embodying the divine feminine—to softening, surrendering, feeling. But I had neglected the part of me who moves forward. The one who protects, who provides structure, who grounds and leads with clarity.

In every partner I had attracted, I was unconsciously searching for the masculine energy I hadn't yet cultivated within myself.

And that's when everything started to shift. Not because someone new arrived. But because I did. I began making decisions based on alignment rather than fear. I stopped waiting for someone else's validation and started listening to my body. I gave myself the consistency I had spent years hoping others would provide.

The more I did that, the less I needed anyone else to fill the gaps— because I had become the one who stayed. I was no longer outsourcing safety. I am no longer running from my own needs. I no longer abandoned my femininity just to be held by someone who couldn't even hold myself.

And that changed everything. The more I trusted my inner masculine, the more my feminine softened—not in fear, but in freedom. I had become the container. The anchor. The presence I had always longed for.

And that's when the obsession faded. Not because the connection lost its meaning but because I no longer needed it to prove something I had already reclaimed within myself.

The Twin Flame Mirror: It's Not Personal—It's Precise

It's easy to take it personally. When they ghost you. When they run from the very love they claimed to want. When they shut down just as you're opening your heart, or act like the connection never existed at all. In those moments, the mind starts spinning stories. *If I was more healed, they'd stay. If I didn't trigger them, we'd be together. If I could just be less emotional, they'd come closer. If I was enough, they wouldn't leave.*

But what if none of this is personal? What if the twin-flame journey was never about being chosen—but about being mirrored?

Because your twin doesn't just trigger you. They reflect you. Not necessarily your personality but your energy. They illuminate the unhealed pieces, the forgotten parts, the internal dynamics that have been running beneath the surface for years—maybe even lifetimes.

When they abandon you, they're showing you where you still leave yourself. When they don't commit, they're reflecting your own fear of fully choosing your truth. When they ignore your needs, they're mirroring how often you've dismissed your own. And when they disappear, they're offering you an invitation to finally reappear—to yourself.

This isn't a punishment. It's precision. Energetic intelligence at work. A soul-designed feedback loop that continually points you back—not toward them, but inward.

And when you stop resisting the reflection… when you stop making their behavior mean something about your worth… when you stop trying to fix them and start listening to what your own energy is trying to reveal—that's when everything begins to shift.

You begin to see you're not being rejected. You're being redirected. Redirected toward the parts of you still waiting to be seen, felt, loved, and reclaimed.

The obsessive longing that once felt like suffering becomes a sacred trail back to your own unmet needs. The emotional spirals that once left you doubting your progress become invitations to stay present with your pain instead of running from it. The silence that once felt like abandonment becomes the stillness where your soul can finally find its voice.

Because the mirror of your twin flame isn't here to tell you who to become for them—they're here to remind you of the parts of yourself you've forgotten how to be.

And the more you recognize the reflection without reacting to it, the more power you call back. Because instead of reaching outward for validation, you begin to root deeper within yourself—into clarity, into choice, into truth.

The Wounded Feminine: When Receptivity Becomes Self-Abandonment

This isn't about gender—it's about energy. The feminine lives in all of us. It's the part that feels, receives, creates, nurtures, and longs to be deeply met. When healthy, this energy is intuitive, grounded, emotionally aware, and naturally magnetic. It trusts. It listens. It softens without collapsing. It attracts—not by force, but by simply being present.

But when the feminine is wounded, that same openness becomes entangled in fear. Receptivity turns into waiting. Emotional depth turns into emotional overwhelm. The desire to be loved becomes a pattern of shrinking, silencing, and self-abandonment in exchange for crumbs of connection.

151

Wounded feminine energy waits—not because of trust, but because of fear. Fear that asking for what's needed will push love away. Fear that speaking truth will be too much. Fear that taking up space will lead to rejection. So the energy begins to contract—giving more than it receives, suppressing truth to keep the peace, and trusting signs and synchronicities more than its own body.

It may show up as overextending to stay connected. Staying silent in hopes of being seen. Romanticizing inconsistency as spiritual growth. Longing for validation, but unsure how to receive it. Regardless of how it appears, the root pattern is the same: abandoning self in hopes of being chosen.

The wounded feminine doesn't just ache—it internalizes the pain and spiritualizes it. It turns longing into a ritual. It calls waiting sacred. But what it really needs is not more signs, more silence, or more surrender. What it needs is to be witnessed. Not fixed. Not dismissed. Just fully felt.

This is where the inner masculine must rise. The part of the self that grounds, holds, protects and says with presence: *"You are safe here. I've got you."* Not from a place of fixing—but from a place of unwavering support.

Because when wounded feminine energy leads, it often appears to be surrender on the surface—but underneath, it's a survival strategy. It's not the truth. It's a pattern. And the answer isn't to reject this part. The answer is to love it back into wholeness.

Under the waiting is wisdom. Beneath the ache is power. Beneath the fear lies the core longing to feel safe and be fully expressed.

That's what the feminine within truly desires—not to be chosen or saved—but to be held, honored, and free. Not because it did something right. Not because the connection came back. But because it is finally remembered, worth isn't proven through pain.

It was never about being seen by someone else. It was about being safe enough to know the self.

The Unavailable Masculine: The Protector That Forgot to Stay

This isn't about men. It's about masculine energy—an inner force we all carry, regardless of identity. The masculine is the part that leads with clarity, takes action from alignment, creates structure, and protects what matters. It's the presence that holds, the consistency that calms, the discernment that grounds. When this energy is healthy, it becomes the inner anchor. It stays. It shows up. It makes space for emotion without trying to fix it. It moves with purpose but stays rooted in presence.

But when the masculine is wounded, it becomes unavailable. It avoids. It distracts. It stays in motion to outrun the discomfort of emotion. It numbs out instead of tuning in. It chooses control over connection, logic over presence, and silence over softness. And not because it's broken—but because, at some point, avoiding felt safer than staying.

When this pattern is internalized, it may manifest as an over-controlling life rather than trusting the flow. It may manifest as a deep distrust of feelings, relying solely on strategy and reason. It might seem like the one who holds everything together for everyone else—but forgets how to hold space for their own needs. The nervous system remains on high alert, always active, and never at rest because resting would mean feeling. And feeling feels unsafe.

The wounded masculine resists vulnerability because softness has been misunderstood as a sign of weakness. It prefers to plan, perfect, and produce—but cannot often pause. And when this energy runs unconsciously within, it's easy to project it outward. Suddenly, the external world reflects this same dynamic back: partners who can't commit, connections that disappear, people who show up in words but not in presence.

It's tempting to ask, "Why won't they stay?" But the more powerful question is, "Where have I stopped staying with myself?"

Because the inner feminine doesn't just want to feel—she wants to feel safe to feel. She wants to know that when emotions rise, something steady will be there to hold them. Not silence. Not suppression. Not disappearance. Presence.

And that presence has to come from within.

Reclaiming the inner masculine isn't about pushing harder or suppressing emotion. It's not about effort. It's about embodiment. Becoming the energetic container that holds space for all of you. Protecting your truth. Acting on your knowing. Following through on the promises you make to yourself. Not outsourcing stability to someone else's readiness—but becoming the sacred structure your own being can trust.

Because when your inner masculine is awake and aligned, everything shifts. You stop abandoning the self to chase safety outside of you. You stop waiting for someone to hold you—and start rising as the one who knows how to stay.

Not because it's easy. But because it's who you've always been underneath the avoidance. The one who leads with love protects with presence and stands in truth—not for applause, but for alignment.

That is a sacred union within. And it changes everything.

The Abandoned Inner Child: Where It All Begins

Long before you met your twin flame… before the spiral of longing, the ache of obsession, or the deep pull toward connection… you met something else: rejection. It didn't always come in dramatic waves. Sometimes, it arrived quietly. A parent who showed up physically but checked out emotionally. A caregiver who praised your achievements but dismissed your tears. A moment when you dared to speak your truth—and it was too much for someone else to hold.

And in that moment, something imprinted deep within you: *"I must not be lovable as I am."*

That's where it began. The fracture. The moment your inner child stopped trusting their emotions. The moment love shifted from something natural to something that had to be earned. Silence started to feel safer than truth. Hiding became a survival strategy. And the real abandonment didn't start with them—it started when you abandoned yourself.

You stopped asking for what you needed. You started performing to be loved. You learned to be good, quiet, strong, and helpful—because those roles got approval. But they came at a cost: the loss of your most honest, untamed, and authentic self.

Then, the twin flame arrives. The soul mirror. The one who awakens you activates you and makes you feel more alive than you ever have before. The intensity is otherworldly. The love feels destined. But when they pull away—when they go silent, ghost, or disappear—it's not just the adult you who feels that loss. It's the inner child. The one who still fears being too much. The one who still aches to be chosen. The one who internalized love as a reward for performance, not a birthright.

This is why the spiral hits so hard. Why the obsession feels like survival. Why the nervous system erupts, even when the mind understands what's happening. This moment is activating a much older wound—the wound of not feeling safe to simply exist and be loved exactly as you are.

This is the root. The original rupture. The reason the feminine energy within struggles to receive is that the masculine energy within stays in constant motion. The reason familiar patterns feel magnetic, even when they hurt. This is the part of you that doesn't need the twin flame to return.

It needs *you*.

It needs you to stay when the emotions rise. To listen when the truth feels uncomfortable. To stop abandoning your body, your voice, and your needs every time love feels like it might leave. This isn't about fixing the past—it's about being present in the now. That is the essence of reparenting.

Reparenting isn't a concept. It's a choice. A practice. A return. It's about choosing to respond differently in the moments when you'd typically run, remain silent, or self-sacrifice. It's becoming the steady presence your inner child never had. The one who says: *"I see you. I hear you. I will not leave you again."*

Because your twin flame wasn't the source of the pain—they were the spotlight. A catalyst that illuminated the tenderness already buried inside. And now, you have the chance to become what no one else ever was: the safe place, the loving protector, the unshakable home your inner child has always needed.

This is where healing begins. And it's how wholeness is restored.

The Return to Wholeness: Tools to Reparent, Reclaim, and Reunite

Healing the mirror isn't about fixing what's broken—it's about returning to what is whole. Reclaiming the parts of you you've abandoned, denied, or hidden just to feel safe or loved. The part that still waits to be chosen. The one who's terrified to feel too much. The one who overfunctions, overgives, or overperforms because somewhere deep inside, love still feels conditional.

This isn't just about insight. It's about embodiment. About safety. About building an inner sanctuary where your emotions are allowed to exist without being ridiculed. The following tools aren't here to get you over your twin flame—they're here to guide you towards inner union.

Start with the mirror. Carve out 10–15 minutes of uninterrupted space. Let your journal become a safe space for your inner child to express itself. Ask: *What does my inner child need from me right now—emotionally, physically, or spiritually?* Reflect on the ways you may still be abandoning yourself in an attempt to earn love. Where do you silence your truth to be accepted, desired, or chosen? What would it feel like to become the masculine energy you keep seeking in others? Don't rush these answers. They won't come from your head—they'll rise from your nervous system.

Then, meet yourself in the mirror. Stand tall. Breathe deeply. Look into your own eyes—not just as you are now, but as you were then... back when love first felt unsafe. Place your hand on your heart and say aloud, "I see you. I believe you. I will not leave you again. You are safe with me. You matter. You are more than enough." Say it until you soften. Say it until something inside you exhales. This is what reparenting looks like—not just words, but presence. Not just affirmation but repair.

Each day, activate your sacred inner masculine. Start your morning grounded. One hand on your heart. One on your belly. Breathe. Drop into your core. Speak this out loud: "Today, I lead from love—not fear. I take aligned action on behalf of my wholeness. I am safe to trust myself." And then—follow through. Say no when your body says no. Speak up when the truth rises, even if your voice shakes. Take the next step you've been avoiding. This is how your masculine rebuilds trust with your feminine—not with promises, but with presence, not with control, but with commitment.

And when you need a reminder, carry this mantra with you like sacred medicine: *"I now choose to love all of me—the child, the feeler, the protector, and the truth-teller. I don't need someone to complete me. I am home."* Whisper it. Breathe it. Let it echo through your cells until it becomes the new frequency of your life.

Because healing isn't about perfection. It's about reunion.

And now—you are the one who gets to stay.

The Mirror Was Never the Problem—It Was the Portal

For so long, you thought the pain came from them—their silence, their distance, the way they looked straight into your soul and then walked away like it meant nothing. You believed the ache was because of what they did, what they didn't do, how they didn't stay. But now, through all the spirals and stillness, you're starting to see what was really being shown.

They weren't exposing your flaws. They were mirroring the places within you, still longing for your own presence, permission, and love.

That obsession you felt? It wasn't madness or weakness—it was a signal. A flare from the forgotten parts of you, trying to find their way back through the chaos. The longing that hollowed your chest wasn't about them—it was the echo of your own soul, aching to be witnessed. The heartbreak didn't come to punish you. It came to crack open the illusion that love lives outside of you.

Because your twin flame wasn't the destination. They were the doorway. The mirror. The trigger that surfaced what you've spent a lifetime avoiding: the ache of not being fully with yourself. And when you stopped chasing the image in the mirror, when you stopped trying to perfect the reflection just to feel worthy of love—that's when the real shift happened.

You returned to your center.

You stop outsourcing your peace and start protecting it. You stop reaching out and start reaching in. You don't stop loving—you stop abandoning. You stop filtering your truth to be accepted and start honoring your full expression. You stop performing healing for the sake of reunion and start embodying it for the sake of your own freedom.

This was never about fixing the reflection. It was about finally seeing yourself clearly through it. And now that you have, you're free—not from love, but from the illusion that you ever had to lose yourself to find it.

The real reunion was never about them returning. It was about re-claiming the version of you who knows how to hold your own heart. To see the child who still wants to be seen. To become the protector who's learning how to stay. To embody the wholeness that never left, even when the people you loved did.

This isn't about forgetting them. This is about remembering all the parts of yourself that you've disconnected from in your quest to be enough.

Because the mirror? It was never the enemy. It was the portal to your wholeness. And you, love—you just walked through it.

Part Four

Becoming the One

CHAPTER 10
STOP SEARCHING. START ATTRACT-ING

*The love I've been waiting for is already within
me.*

You've done the work. Faced the mirror. Released the cords. Reclaimed the energy. You've felt the ache of letting go and the quiet power of returning to yourself. And now, something is shifting. Not out there—but in you.

Because even after all the rituals and reminders, all the signs and surrender, there's still a tension beneath it all. A silent pressure to "get it right." A subtle waiting for the connection to finally click, the timing to align, and the reward to arrive.

But here's what not many understand: sometimes, the waiting becomes the block. The constant search sends one message to the Universe—"It's not here yet." The Universe is always faithful to reflect your frequency and simply responds, "Okay."

This chapter marks the end of the pattern.

Not because you've mastered manifesting. But because you've stopped chasing what you already are. The truth is, you don't attract from desire—you attract from identity. From embodiment. From the frequency you hold when no one is watching.

You've been trying to prove you're ready. But readiness isn't a performance. It's a presence.

You attract love when you stop outsourcing your wholeness and start *being* the vibration you've been seeking. Because you're not missing anything. You're not waiting on timing, worthiness, or divine approval. You're here to remember that you are the source.

And when you live like love is already here, it doesn't need to be summoned—it simply meets you. Not because you searched harder… but because you finally stopped searching.

I Didn't Find the Flame— I Became It

I always thought becoming magnetic meant perfecting something. Healing every layer. Fixing every flaw. Aligning so precisely with love that the Universe would finally reward me with "the one." I thought magnetism was about manifesting the flame.

But the truth is… I had to *become* it.

The day I left Sedona, I didn't know what I was walking away from— or what I was walking toward. I just knew something was complete. I had closed out a chapter that had both broken me and built me. That desert had seen me at my worst, at my rawest, at my most stripped bare. It had also been the womb of my rebirth.

That same day, a fellow transformational teacher and spiritual mentor reached out to me. He was local to Sedona and also an author. He invited me to coffee. I told him, "I'd love to… but I just left Sedona, and I'm not sure when I'll be back."

We had never met before—even though we'd been neighbors. We shared the same circles and walked the talk, yet somehow, our paths never crossed. I assumed he was reaching out to collaborate. From the outside, it looked like we were walking the same mission.

Months later, as I prepared to return to Sedona, he commented on one of my posts. I replied, letting him know I'd be back soon and that we could get together if he was still interested in connecting. We did. But it wasn't about business. It turned out he wasn't looking to collaborate—he was curious about me.

He invited me to dinner. The connection was easy, fun, and unexpected. As we began to talk more, something became clear: I wasn't the same woman who had once yearned to be chosen. I wasn't looking for a relationship—I was focused on getting to know the woman I had become and building a relationship with myself first. I told him this up front. That I wanted to date differently. Consciously. Slowly. That I wasn't here to fall into another combustion of spiritual intensity and trauma bonding. I wanted to discover who someone *really was* beyond the connection. Beyond the spark. What they valued. Where they were going. What kind of life they were building and whether that life aligned with mine.

And something amazing happened—he met me there. No pressure. No pursuit. No pushing.

We began to explore a different kind of intimacy—one born of presence, not urgency. Curiosity, not possession. We both had done our work. He was rooted in his divine masculine. I was resting in my healed feminine. There was no chasing, no testing, no one needing to be rescued. Just two sovereign souls walking side by side, exploring what it means to *be* without needing to become anything for the other.

I told him I didn't know where my life was leading me. That I am in a gap: the space between who I was and who I'm becoming. He said maybe he was the bridge—not to save me, but to walk beside me as I cross into what I now know I deserve. There were no strings. Just safety. No roles. Just respect. We didn't need to talk about spiritual concepts—we were too busy *living* them. Laughing. Eating. Hiking. Resting. Playing. Being human again after years of spiritual survival mode.

And for the first time, I saw it clearly: I had become the man I always dreamed of. Because he showed up as my mirror. The mirror of my mission. My wholeness. My healed masculine. And I no longer *needed* him to complete anything in me—because I was already full.

This wasn't a fantasy. This wasn't a twin-flame illusion. This was *real*. Grounded. Present. Sacred in its simplicity. It felt like a *spiritual escape into the physical world*—where love didn't need to be labeled or controlled but could simply be experienced.

He calls himself a healer of the divine feminine. But what's beautiful is that he doesn't have to heal *me*. And I don't have to fix his masculinity. We're both whole. We're both free. And in that freedom, we're exploring something so rare—a connection without pressure, attachment, or expectation. Just the daily decision to show up as we are and see what's alive.

We've even talked about writing a book together. Something he saw us doing before I did. Something that reflects the kind of interactions we're co-creating—a synergy that rises *not* from the wounds but from the ashes.

Because that's what this season is. I didn't just become magnetic. I became the flame. Not because someone finally chose me. But because I finally stopped searching outside myself. I became my own fire. My own light. My own warrior lover, which is what I call him.

This is the beauty in the ashes.
This is the phoenix rising.
This is what happens when you stop chasing—and start *embodying*.

The Frequency of Lack: Why Searching Keeps You Separate
Searching feels like action. Like dedication. Like a commitment to the vision. But energetically, it's a declaration of absence. The more you look for love "out there," the more your field echoes the message: "It's not here." Every time you revisit old conversations, linger in memories or seek confirmation from the Universe, you're signaling one thing: *I'm still not whole. I'm still hoping something outside of me will fill in what's missing.* I still need something outside of me to feel okay.

164

Manifesting is not about what you say—it's about what your energy communicates. And the Universe doesn't respond to words. It responds to frequency. You could be doing all the "right" spiritual things—rituals, visualizations, mantras—but if the root of those actions is lacking, the field will simply reflect it back.

This is why the seeking becomes a trap. Because the more you search, the further love feels. The more you grasp, the more it slips through your hands. The more you try to manifest from desperation, the more delayed your desire becomes—not as punishment, but as energetic precision. Love can't land where it's being chased. It needs space to meet you. It needs stability to respond. It requires a self-sourced frequency to recognize what you are asking for.

You're not unworthy. You're not broken. But if your actions are fueled by a belief that you're not whole yet. Therefore, the outcomes will echo that same emptiness.

So, instead of getting anxious because what you're asking for isn't showing up, pause and breathe. Come back to your body.

And drop the rituals performed from fear. Stop checking for confirmation. Feel into the space beneath the grasping—the place where your soul already knows that *nothing is missing.* In that space, something new emerges. A steady pulse. A quiet power. The remembrance that you are already more than enough.

Because attraction doesn't happen through effort. It occurs through embodiment.

When you stop sending out "please come love me" energy… and start pulsing "I am love, I am whole, and I am safe to be seen"—that's when everything begins to shift. That's when the waiting ends. That's when the loop dissolves. Not because someone else returned to claim you —but because you reclaimed yourself.

Magnetism Over Mechanics: The Power of Embodied Feminine Wholeness

The healed feminine doesn't chase. She doesn't perform, convince, or manipulate timelines through rituals or strategies. She doesn't wait for a text to confirm her worth or twist herself into someone else's fantasy to feel chosen. She knows she's already enough. And that knowing—deep, steady, embodied—creates an energetic field that pulls in what's aligned without needing to reach for it.

Magnetism is feminine energy at rest, yet completely alive. Present. Potent. Undeniable.

However, let's make one thing clear: this has nothing to do with gender. Feminine energy lives in all of us. It's the part of you that receives. That listens without rushing to fix. That feels without apologizing. That surrenders—not from weakness, but from a profound trust in your own essence.

When this energy is wounded, it clings. It waits. It over-functions. It gives everything while asking for little, hoping someone will intuit the ache underneath the silence and return it with love. The wounded feminine doesn't trust that her presence is enough, so she tries harder, reaches more, and loses herself in the process.

But when the feminine is healed? She no longer tries to be seen. She *is* the vision.

She doesn't need to chase love—she becomes the frequency of it. She honors her truth without explanation. She moves through life with a quiet confidence that speaks louder than any performance. Her presence becomes a transmission: "I am here. I am whole. I am open—but only to what honors me."

That's when magnetism comes online.

It's not something you perform. It's not a pose. It's not a perfectly timed post or a curated ritual designed to call them back. It's what happens when you turn your energy inward and build your life around your own essence.

This kind of energy shows up in the subtlest yet most powerful ways. You don't fill silence out of discomfort. You rest in it, and the room shifts around your stillness. Your boundaries aren't walls— they're invitations to meet you in a deeper, safer, more honest way.

You prioritize pleasure not to be indulgent but because you understand that aligned love responds to aliveness. You don't prove you're ready. You embody it.

When you live from this place, something radical happens: you stop craving. You start creating. You stop needing to be picked. You start choosing yourself. And your frequency begins to say what your mouth no longer needs to: "If it's aligned, I welcome it. If it's not, I release it." You stop panicking when timelines shift. You no longer collapse when someone pulls away from you. You know that what's meant for you won't miss you—and you don't have to grip to receive it.

True magnetism cannot be faked. It's not another tool in the manifestation toolbox. It's the natural byproduct of being rooted in your body, your truth, and your worth. It arises when your energy stops leaking out into longing and starts anchoring into presence. It's the energy of a person who's no longer searching—because they've become what they were always trying to find.

You don't become magnetic by being perfect. You become magnetic by being *home*—in yourself.

And nothing attracts love, opportunity, and miracles faster than someone who has already chosen themselves first.

You Are the Signal: The Shift from Seeking to Sourcing

I didn't realize how much of my energy was wired for searching. Not just for *him*—but for *them*. For the next spark, the next sign, the next hit of hope that maybe this time, the connection would hold. Perhaps this time, it would feel safe enough to stay. I wasn't just chasing a person—I was chasing the feeling I got when someone else's attention temporarily quieted the ache inside me. That fleeting moment when their presence made me feel seen. Validated. Enough.

It wasn't about a single relationship. It was about a lifetime of dynamics that mirrored the same wound. A pattern of reaching for something outside of me to reflect what I hadn't yet claimed within. Each time they pulled away, the emptiness returned louder. Each time they went silent, so did my center. When I first began anchoring into my divine feminine, there was a part of me that instinctively longed for the sacred masculine to come in and hold me. To offer protection, stability, and security—a safe place to land after so many lifetimes of doing it all myself. I wanted to be met, held, and supported by a presence strong enough to make me feel safe.

But what I had to learn—what cracked me open in the most profound way—was that those things weren't coming from outside of me. I wasn't waiting for a man to make me feel grounded. I was being called to become that for myself. To awaken the masculine energy within me that could create structure around my softness. To embody the presence, the protector, the provider I had spent so long looking for in someone else.

And once I found that in myself? Everything changed. I didn't just feel safe. I felt sovereign. I no longer needed someone to hold me up because I was already standing fully in my own center.

What I finally came to see was that obsession isn't really about another person—it's about disconnection from self. It's what happens when the inner child still believes that love lives outside of us when they haven't yet learned that *they* are the source. That was the shift I didn't realize I was being called to make. Not from unhealed to healed. But from seeking love outside of me to sourcing it from within.

And when I began to source from within, everything changed. I stopped pulling cards to get clarity. I stopped asking mentors what it meant. I stopped chasing external signs to feel a sense of connection. Because I had become the oracle. The answers were no longer outside of me—they were arising from within. Just like the message behind my *Twin Flame Ascension: Take Me Home* oracle deck, I had taken myself home.

I wasn't reading energy—I was embodying it.

Instead of asking the Universe for confirmation, I asked myself, *"What would it feel like to embody the frequency of love right now— even if nothing outside of me changed?"*

I stopped waiting to be chosen and started choosing myself—in every moment, with every breath, through every small act of reverence that whispered, *"I'm enough, just as I am."*

It wasn't about shutting down or silencing my feelings. It was about finally honoring them. I didn't need to escape the longing—I needed to listen to what it was trying to teach me. Every craving, every ache, every moment of reaching outside myself became an invitation to return inward. To stop abandoning my own needs in search of someone else's presence. To stop leaking power into the past and start anchoring it into the present—into me.

And here's what I came to embody: when you become the source, you stop attracting from a place of lack. You no longer send out the signal of "Come complete me," but instead radiate, *"I'm whole. I'm grounded. I'm home."* And that frequency? It's magnetic. That's when attraction becomes effortless—not because you stopped desiring love, but because you finally became the embodiment of it.

So, I stopped lighting candles for someone who wasn't lighting up my life. I stopped scripting the future with a partner who wasn't present in my reality. And instead of asking the Universe to deliver someone new, I started asking myself harder questions: *Am I truly living like someone who believes they are already loved? Am I setting boundaries like someone who knows their worth? Am I creating a life so rich, so true, that only a partner operating at the same frequency could even find me?*

That's what alignment really looks like. Not perfection. Not another vision board. But radical self-honesty. It means no longer confusing intensity with intimacy. It means choosing the relationship that brings peace to your nervous system, not chaos to your soul. It means being willing to let go of the people, patterns, and past versions of yourself that once needed drama to feel alive.

Because aligned love doesn't enter through the backdoor of confusion. It walks through the front door of clarity. It's not about summoning a soulmate with smoke and moonlight. It's about becoming someone who can hold sacred connections without losing themselves in the process. When you live in alignment, you don't have to chase it. You *attract* it—because you *are* it.

And that means making different choices—before the relationship arrives. You stop romanticizing inconsistency. You stop confusing longing with depth. You stop bending your boundaries in hopes that love will land more softly. You learn to listen to your body. You honor your no's as sacred. You treat your energy field like the altar it is—only letting in what aligns with your wholeness.

That's the shift. Not from single to couple. But from leaking energy to leading it. From waiting to becoming. From trying to manifest love to magnetizing it—because you've become the energetic match for what you've asked for.

I started living differently after I made that shift. I began each morning by asking myself: *If I were already in a sacred partnership, how would I navigate this day?* Not because I was trying to pretend—but because I was embodying. I no longer needed someone else to validate my worth. I was living in alignment with it. I stopped auditioning for connection and started anchoring into coherence. Because the version of me who's met in divine love? She's not grasping. She's grounded. She's not chasing. She's clear. And that clarity became the call.

Because here's what no one tells you: the partner you're meant to share your path with isn't looking for chaos to save. They're looking for someone who's already holding their own frequency. They're drawn to your embodiment, not your effort to your alignment, not your anxiety.

So, if you really want to call in the one who matches your mission, don't focus on finding them. Focus on becoming the you they'll recognize. The you who doesn't perform or pretend. The you who doesn't hide behind spiritual language or emotional fantasy. The you who knows their worth live their purpose and trusts their own timing.

And when that moment comes—when presence meets presence, when energy meets energy—you won't feel like you've been rescued. You'll feel like you've been seen. Not because they arrived. But because you finally saw yourself.

Magnetizing From the Inside Out: Tools to Live the Frequency of Love

Magnetism isn't a vibe you turn on once you feel better. It's a frequency you embody in the moments you're most tempted to spiral. Not when it's easy—but exactly when your nervous system is screaming for a hit of validation, attention, or hope.

These tools aren't here to help you "get" the person.

They're here to help you become the person who no longer needs to chase—because you've already come home to yourself.

Self-Rescue in Real Time: The Spiral Reset

This practice is designed for the exact moment your energy starts to slip.

The scroll. The stalk. The second-guessing. The obsession.

1. **Name the Pattern**
   o Say aloud: *"This is a moment I used to abandon myself. But now, I choose to stay."*
2. **Breathe into Safety**
   o Place one hand on your heart and the other on your belly.
   o Inhale for 4... hold for 2... exhale for 6. Repeat three times.
3. **Interrupt the Urge**
   o Ask:
      ▪ What part of me is activated right now?
      ▪ What would I be giving them right now that I could give to me?
4. **Redirect with Ritual**

- o Move your body outside—even if just for five minutes.
- o Write a letter from your Higher Self to your inner child.
- o Turn on one song that makes you feel *sexy, sacred, or sovereign*—and dance until your energy comes back online.

Embodiment Activation: Future Self Frequency

Every day, for five minutes, live as if your divine partnership already exists.

1. **Visualize the Future You**
   - o See the version of you who is fully met, fully seen, and fully thriving in sacred love.
2. **Ask Them:**
   - o *What do you want me to remember today?*
   - o *What do you no longer tolerate?*
   - o *What do you embody now that I'm ready to step into?*
3. **Act As If**
   - o Eat like them. Walk like them. Dress like them.
   - o Speak boundaries like them.
   - o Make one choice they would already feel safe making.

This bridges the gap between where you are and who you're becoming.

Energetic Hygiene for Love Attraction

Your energy is your dating profile. Keep it clean.

Place your hands on your body—heart and womb, or heart and solar plexus.

Say aloud:

> *"I call my power back from everywhere I've left it.*
> *I release what no longer reflects my truth.*
> *I fill this space with my essence. I am home."*

Visualize a golden sphere surrounding you, pulsing with your own radiant frequency.

Do this daily. Especially when you've been spinning, spiraling, or sourcing externally.

Affirmation to Anchor the Flame

"I no longer seek love. I am love.
I no longer chase alignment. I embody it.
I am not waiting—I am already the flame."

Say it in the mirror. Say it when you're triggered. Say it when your energy needs to remember who you are.

Because magnetism doesn't come from being chosen.

It comes from choosing yourself—again and again—until it becomes your baseline.

You Don't Have to Find the Flame—You Already Are It

The twin-flame journey doesn't begin with a fairytale. It starts with fire. With the kind of pain that scorches everything you thought love was supposed to be. The type of loss that doesn't just break your heart—it burns down your identity. The connection you swore was your destiny turned into the initiation you never saw coming. And somewhere between the obsession and the letting go, the waiting and the waking up, everything you weren't meant to carry got reduced to ash.

But that was never the end. That was the rebirth.

Because you don't become the flame by finding the one.

You become the flame by walking through everything that tried to extinguish you—and you stayed lit.

Not because it didn't hurt. Not because you didn't want to be chosen. But because you finally stopped abandoning yourself in the name of love. You stopped waiting for someone else to rise... and you rose anyway. Shaky. Sacred. Sovereign.

This is why most people are reluctant to face genuine healing. It's not polished. It's not always pretty. It's messy. It's raw. It's standing in the rubble of everything that once defined you and choosing to rebuild from discernment, not delusion. From inner alignment, not emotional negotiation. No longer bending your truth to keep the hope alive, but standing in it—even if it means standing alone. Choosing mutual energy. A consistent effort. And the connection that doesn't require you to lose yourself to feel loved.

When I stopped waiting to be chosen, I met a version of myself I had never known. Not the one performing for love. But the one pulsing with it. I no longer needed to be found. I *was* the source. The warmth. The light. The signal.

So, if you're still wondering when they'll return when it makes sense for the pain to finally mean something—pause. Because that focus is what keeps you from seeing the magic.

You are the aftermath.
You are the alchemy.
You walked through the fire.
You stood in the wreckage.

And you didn't just survive.
You transmuted.
Into the light.
The heat.
The clarity.
The frequency of truth itself.

You're not waiting to become whole.
You're walking proof that wholeness was never lost.

Because when you stop chasing what's inconsistent, when you stop shape-shifting to stay chosen, when you stop outsourcing your worth—you stop broadcasting longing. You start pulsing power. You don't hope to be seen. You become unforgettable.

And that, my friend, will make you magnetic AF. 🔯

CHAPTER 11
LOVE BEYOND THE LABEL

I don't need a label to claim who I am.

There was a time when I clung to the twin-flame label as if it were a lifeline. It felt sacred, cosmic, otherworldly as if the Universe had finally given me a definition for the fire I couldn't explain. Every sign, every synchronicity, every ache suddenly made sense. I wasn't just heartbroken; I was awakening. I wasn't just longing; I was in preparation for union. And for a while, that story gave me something to hold onto—until the label that once felt like truth started to feel like a trap.

The deeper I went into the twin-flame narrative, the more I realized how much of it wasn't mine. I had inherited the framework, the stages, the roles. The runner. The chaser. The divine masculine. The separation. I began to shape my healing around timelines I didn't create and expectations I didn't question. I stopped asking myself how I actually felt in the connection—and started asking what phase we were in. I didn't walk away when it hurt because twin flames "trigger your growth." I didn't set boundaries because pain was supposed to be part of the process. And somewhere in that madness of spiritual logic, I started abandoning my own truth.

Because when you label yourself, you begin to live by the rules of the label. You don't just say you're a twin flame—you start to code your entire nervous system with what you believe that means. And so often, those beliefs aren't soul-deep. They're trauma-deep. Woven from other people's pain. Shaped by the collective ache of seekers just trying to make sense of the intensity. You tell yourself this must be love because it feels impossible to let go. You hold on, not because your soul says stay, but because your identity is tied to the label.

But what if the love that cracked you open wasn't meant to be labeled at all?

What if the real purpose of that connection wasn't to teach you who your twin flame was but to show you who *you* are? What if you've been calling pain a portal when your soul is simply asking you to release the story?

This chapter isn't about rejecting the experience. It's about reclaiming your voice inside it. It's about peeling away the spiritual vocabulary and asking: *What do I actually know to be true—beyond the label?* It's an invitation to step outside the template, not to invalidate what happened, but to liberate the parts of you that still feel stuck because of what you called it.

Because maybe they were your twin flame. Or perhaps they weren't. Maybe they were a soul mirror, a karmic ignition, a divine disruptor sent to shake you awake. Or perhaps the "who" no longer matters—because the real journey is not about naming the love. It's about becoming the one who can live it. Freely. Fully. Without cages. Without conditions. Without needing a label to give it meaning.

And that journey starts here.

When I Realized I Was the Label

I used to think that letting go of the label meant giving up on love. On *the* love. The one that cracked me open. The one I believed was my twin flame. But over time—through heartbreak, healing, and the arrival of new soul reflections—I came to understand something much more profound: I wasn't actually chasing a man. I was chasing meaning. And for a long time, I believed the label *was* the meaning.

The twin-flame title gave me something to hold onto. A structure. A sacred storyline to make sense of the intensity I was feeling. But eventually, that label became the very thing that limited me. It kept me from expanding into the fullness of who I was becoming. It stopped me from seeing what else could be possible, who else could come in, and what other aspects of myself were still waiting to be mirrored back.

Because when you're so focused on proving someone is your twin flame, you stop asking yourself what your soul actually needs. You stop listening to how the connection actually feels. You override your own clarity in favor of a collective narrative—and that's when the pain begins to loop.

Once I let go of the need for it to be *him*, something powerful happened. Life began sending in higher reflections—souls who met me at the level of healing I had integrated. Men who showed me new layers of love, truth, and wholeness. But I wouldn't have seen them—let alone received them—if I had still been gripping the old story with white-knuckled hope.

The label had become a box. One that told me this was the ultimate love and anything else would be less than that. But that box was built on outdated beliefs, spiritual fairytales, and collective projections that weren't even mine. Inside it, I was shrinking. Because I had equated the label with my identity. And when you do that, you start living by the rules of the label instead of the wisdom of your soul.

What I discovered, and what I now teach, is this: *I* was the label. The connection I was craving wasn't with a person—it was with the parts of myself I thought I could only access through them. The love, the fire, the awakening—it was never just about the person. It was about the spiritual process taking place inside of me.

When I dropped the label, I didn't lose the love. I expanded it. I stopped limiting myself to one person as the sole source of transformation. I stopped making pain sacred just because it was intense. I stopped organizing my entire life around someone else's absence. And in that space, I made room for something new. Something deeper. Something that grew *with* me, not something that kept me trapped in who I used to be.

The truth is that when you cling to a label, you limit your own evolution. You block the arrival of new reflections that can help you see even more of who you are. The label becomes a ceiling—and your soul wants a sky. Letting go doesn't mean the love wasn't real. It means you're finally ready for love that's aligned, expansive, and alive in the now. A love that meets you in your power—not in your longing. And once you stop trying to make the story fit the label, you open the door to something even greater: a connection that reflects your wholeness, not your wounds.

Why Releasing the Label Sets You Free

Letting go of the label wasn't just an emotional turning point for me—it was a spiritual liberation. And while I didn't know it at the time, I was breaking free from more than just a story. I was freeing myself from three significant limitations that were holding me back:

1. The label became a ceiling instead of a compass.

It narrowed my growth. It told me this was *the one*, so I missed the higher reflections who showed up to mirror who I was becoming.

2. The label kept me stuck in obsession instead of embodiment.

It made me think if I worked harder, healed deeper, or surrendered better, I'd earn the outcome. It turned love into a performance.

3. The label distorted the meaning of the journey.

I thought the pain proved the connection. But all it really did was prove how far I had disconnected from myself.

This journey was never about earning someone back. It was about remembering who I am. And once I reclaimed that… everything changed.

What Happens When You Stay Attached to the Identity?

The label becomes the cage—when the identity overshadows the love.

In the beginning, the term "twin flame" felt like an awakening. It offered structure to the chaos—the magnetic pull, the soul-level intensity, the uncanny synchronicities that made me question everything I thought I understood about love. Finally, there was a map for the terrain I'd been blindly navigating. At first, the label brought relief. Validation. It felt like sacred language for a connection that had cracked me wide open.

But what I didn't see coming was how quickly that label would become a lens. And then, a limitation.

The more I clung to it, the more I filtered my entire experience through its story. Every silence became "separation." Every return is a "test." I wasn't just interpreting the signs—I was dependent on them. Projecting meaning onto every moment until the connection stopped being something I was living and started being something I was trying to decode.

Without realizing it, I traded my truth for a template.

I stopped asking how I really felt. I stopped listening to what my body was trying to tell me. I began editing my emotions to match the spiritual script I thought I was supposed to follow. And in doing so, I lost the most crucial compass I had—my own knowing.

Because this journey was never about a label. It was about the becoming. And that begins the moment you stop chasing a definition—and start choosing your freedom.

Instead of checking in with how I felt in the relationship, I found myself checking in with the label. I began wondering if we were experiencing the "dark night of the soul" or undergoing "karmic purging." I started filtering my pain through a storyline I didn't write but had come to live by. I wasn't assessing the relationship through the lens of my nervous system—I was interpreting it through the collective mythology of what being a twin flame was supposed to mean.

And that's when the label stopped being a mirror... and became a cage.

Because when your identity is wrapped up in a spiritual label, it becomes harder to recognize when something isn't right. You start tolerating pain because you believe it's part of the process. You excuse emotional unavailability because someone once said, "Separation is necessary for ascension." You override your boundaries because walking away would mean "failing the mission." You stop asking, *Does this love honor me?* And instead, ask, *What phase are we in?*

That's when obsession doesn't just come from the person—it comes from the identity. Because the label turns even the most painful dynamic into something sacred. It convinces you that suffering is a sign of progress. It teaches you to call your exhaustion surrender and your confusion clarity. And before you know it, you're trapped inside a belief system that no longer matches your growth.

I know that feeling intimately. I stayed longer than I should have on more than one occasion. I kept watering a connection that had stopped nourishing me because I believed the label made it divine. I thought that walking away meant I wasn't spiritual enough, committed enough, or awakened enough. But eventually, something inside me whispered the truth I had been avoiding: *This label is no longer leading me to love. It's leading me away from myself.*

And that's when I realized—real love doesn't need a title to be transformative. It doesn't need a role, a phase, or a storyline. It doesn't need to be painful to be sacred. Because sometimes, the person who activates your awakening isn't meant to stay. They're intended to usher in your evolution. To walk you to the edge of your next becoming. And the label? It was never meant to be a life sentence. It was meant to be a bridge.

Letting go of the identity wasn't easy. But it was the most loving thing I've ever done. I didn't have to deny the experience to reclaim my power. I didn't have to make it insignificant to make it sacred. I simply had to tell the truth: *This connection was real. It was profound. And I don't need it to be forever to honor what it gave me.*

I laid the label down—not with bitterness, but with reverence. I set the love free—not to erase it, but to let it breathe beyond the confines of what I thought it had to be. And in doing so, I returned to myself. Because when the label no longer leads the story, your soul finally can. And that's when the real union begins—the one you've been longing for all along. The one with yourself.

What If It's Not Your Twin Flame? Asking the Hardest Question

The number one question I received from clients for years was this: *"Is this my twin flame?"*

And for a while, I could answer it. I *did* answer it. I helped people decode the signs, track the stages, and navigate the runner-chaser dynamic. For a time, that clarity served us. The language gave meaning to the chaos. It offered validation for a connection so powerful it felt like nothing else.

But as time passed—and as we collectively began to wake up—I started to realize something: what we were experiencing wasn't just a relationship. It was quantum entanglement. A soul-level mirror designed to trigger transformation, not confirmation.

Everyone is a mirror. Everyone is walking us home.

And while that doesn't invalidate the intensity of the twin-flame experience, it *does* expand it. Because what we used to think of as a linear path to union has evolved into something much deeper: a return to self. A reclamation of our wholeness. A process of remembering that the reunion was never really about another person—it was about the internal merger of our divine masculine and feminine.

What we went through wasn't wrong. Those stages, that ache, the surrender—it all served a purpose. It was part of our collective evolution. However, we're now being asked to see the bigger picture. To understand that the twin-flame journey was never about waiting for someone to come back. It was about becoming the one who never left.

A question lingered for a long time. Like static in the background—barely audible but always present. Especially in the quiet moments when the signs stopped coming when the pain dragged on longer than it should have when the magic began to feel more like a myth than a miracle.

What if they're not my twin flame?

Most people didn't want to hear that it might not be their twin flame—not because the connection wasn't real —but because letting go of the label can feel like letting go of the meaning, the magic, and the hope. I understood that deeply. It wasn't that I stopped believing in what I was teaching. It was that, over time, something deeper within me began to whisper a quiet truth—one I could no longer ignore:

It no longer felt like love. It felt like chasing—like waiting for something that never quite arrived. Like performing devotion on repeat, hoping that one day, maybe, it would finally be returned.

But that quiet whisper, the one I tried so hard to ignore? It was the beginning of my liberation.

Because the moment I stopped needing to name it, I finally allowed myself to feel it. Not as a fantasy I was gripping onto. Not as an identity I had to protect. But as a portal—a passage that wasn't pointing me toward someone else but leading me back home.

Back to the only union that ever truly mattered: the one within.

But to even entertain that question felt like a betrayal. Betrayal of the signs, the synchronicities, the dreams that once made me feel seen by the Universe. Betrayal of the way their presence cracked me open, how the spiritual connection activated something in me that no one else ever had. If I was wrong about the label, what did that mean for everything I'd experienced? What about the love? What about the pull? What about the awakening?

And yet, the more I asked the question, the more I realized something I hadn't been ready to admit: even if they weren't my twin flame, the love was still real. The connection was still sacred. The growth I experienced in their wake was still valid. I didn't need the label to justify what I had gone through. I didn't need to be "right" to honor the way they reflected back parts of me I had long forgotten how to see.

Maybe they were my twin flame. Perhaps they were a karmic partner with sacred timing. Maybe they were a soul mirror sent to activate my most profound healing. Or they were all of those things at once. Because in all reality, not every twin-flame connection is meant to end in union. Not every soul-shifting experience is intended to become a relationship. Sometimes, the most crucial person in your spiritual journey is the one who sets it in motion—not the one who walks beside you to the end.

And if they weren't my twin flame? That didn't mean I failed. It didn't mean I was foolish. It didn't mean I wasted my time. It meant I was brave enough to open my heart. To love fully. To let myself be transformed. To trust a process I couldn't see the end of—and to keep showing up even when it hurt. That is not something to regret. That's something to be proud of.

Because even if they weren't the label I thought they were, they were still the soul I needed. The mirror that showed me my light. The catalyst that woke me up. The presence that, for a season, helped me remember the parts of myself I had abandoned. And maybe that was the point all along—not to get the label right, but to find the freedom to let go of needing one.

So yes, ask the question, what if they're not my twin flame? Let it shake you. Let it unravel every illusion that was built on fantasy instead of truth. And then—let it set you free. Not from the love. But from the cage you built around it.

Surrendering the Storyline: Letting the Path Reveal Itself

There came a moment when the striving just stopped. Not with a bang. Not with a breakdown. Just a quiet, undeniable clarity: I couldn't keep carrying the weight of a story that was never mine to script. I had confused spiritual pursuit with emotional survival—mistaking effort for alignment and control for clarity.

For a long time, I treated healing like a hustle. As if wholeness was something I had to earn by proving my worth through pain. I didn't realize I was negotiating with the divine—offering my grief in exchange for reunion; my sorrow became a currency, and sacrifice was leverage. I wasn't surrendering. I was bargaining. I was micromanaging my transformation, hoping if I hit all the right milestones, love would finally be delivered with a big red bow. However, healing doesn't work that way. Love doesn't respond to performance. And the soul can't be tricked into peace.

Absolute surrender isn't a poetic pose. It's a fire. It burns down the scaffolding you built around a fantasy. It strips away your illusions, leaving you standing bare in the truth of what *is*. Surrender isn't giving up—it's giving back what was never yours to hold. The timelines. The titles. The task of saving someone else's soul.

What cracked me open wasn't a failure. It was finally facing the truth: I had outgrown the chase. Outgrown the version of love that depended on someone else's return to feel whole. I no longer needed anyone's presence to validate my path. I no longer believed that healing was a transaction to earn love. That realization wasn't soft—it was seismic. And it set me free.

Surrender meant choosing peace over performance. Letting the mystery remain mysterious. It meant leaving space for the unknown and finding God not in a promise fulfilled—but in the presence of the now.

I started reclaiming myself in the smallest ways: uncurated joy. A laugh that didn't need to be justified. A dance in my kitchen without waiting for an update from the Universe. I stopped bracing for signs. I stopped bracing, period.

And as the grip loosened, something miraculous happened: life started flowing again. Not because I mastered the manifestation technique or cracked the twin-flame code—but because I finally stepped out of the waiting room and walked back into my life.

What I've come to understand is this: you don't need a label to validate the depth of a connection. You don't need a title to make it real, sacred, or transformative. Some of the most soul-shifting love stories are never defined, never claimed, never made public—but they still alter everything.

You also don't need a reunion to prove the love was true. The ending—or lack of one—doesn't diminish the impact. The love was real because *you* were real. What you felt, what you saw, what it awakened in you—that's what made it sacred. Not whether it circled back or not.

And you don't need the story to wrap up neatly to extract its meaning. Sometimes, the lesson arrives in the unraveling. Sometimes, the most powerful thing you can do is let the plot dissolve, not because it didn't matter, but because you matter more than the version of you who wrote it.

Letting go is not failure. It's not punishment. It's an initiation. A portal into something more profound—into presence, into power, into peace. It's the moment your soul stops waiting and starts expanding.

And when you stop trying to force love to look the way you imagined it would? That's when the truth reveals itself. It never truly left. Because the love was never just about them.

It was always about you. You were always the destination.

Love Isn't Linear—It's Limitless

There was a time when I believed love would reward me for my spiritual effort. If I could hold the frequency, align my energy, stay soft, stay patient, and keep my heart open—even in pain—then one day, the reunion would come. I thought if I passed the test, the Universe would give me the outcome I craved. But love isn't a transaction. It doesn't operate on cosmic checklists or spiritual formulas. Chasing it with perfect behavior only left me exhausted and burned out.

Because real love isn't earned by enduring pain—it's revealed when you finally stop betraying yourself to keep it.

It wasn't until I stepped away from the path I was forcing that I finally felt the pulse of what love really is. Not a transaction. Not a checklist. Not a prize was handed out for spiritual performance. Love is a wild, living energy—one that often arrives through the back door when you stop guarding the front. It's not summoned by strategy or held hostage by how many hours you've spent healing.

Love doesn't clock in when your shadow work is complete or reward you for spiritual endurance. It moves where there's authenticity. It rises in the places you stop hiding. It enters when your guard comes down—not because you've perfected yourself, but because you've finally let yourself be seen. It finds you the moment you stop performing worthiness and start embodying it.

But here's what most of us miss: the work isn't to fix yourself so someone will love you. The real work is to stop believing you have to. The deepest form of self-love isn't found in striving for perfection—it's found in accepting yourself right where you are. Raw. Real. Unfiltered. No edits. No improvements. No performance. Just presence.

Because when you love yourself here—in the in-between, in the becoming, in the not-there-yet—you send a signal to the Universe louder than any affirmation: I believe I'm worthy of love now. Not later. Not "when I'm healed." Not "when they come back." But now. *As I am!*

That's when the shift happens. That's when love no longer feels like something you have to chase. Because you've finally become the proof. And the Universe can't help but meet you there.

I had to unlearn everything I thought I knew about love. I had to drop the fantasy that it arrives in a neat bow when you've done enough "work." I had to see that some connections are sacred *and* short-lived. Some love stories aren't meant to last—but to launch you into a version of yourself that didn't exist before the fire.

And that's not a failure. That's freedom.

The truth is, the real gift wasn't in whether they came back. It was in who I became when they didn't. I stopped trying to make the moment last forever and started letting it stretch *me*. The ache was real. But so was the awakening. The relationship didn't need to last to change my life—it had already done so. I no longer needed it to make sense. I needed it to make space. For my soul. For my truth. For my power.

That's the miracle no one talks about.

Because love isn't linear. It's not a milestone to reach or a box to check. It's an energy that reveals, refines, and realigns you. It's not bound by time. It's not limited to labels. And it doesn't need to be permanent to be profound.

So, let go of the version of love that only felt safe when it was defined. Let go of the outcome you thought you needed to validate the depth of your feelings. Let go of needing it to return to trust it was real.

Because the only thing that is real is that love was never meant to complete you. It was meant to *ignite* you.

And that, beloved, is limitless.

Sacred Release: Tools for Letting Go Without Losing Yourself

Letting go doesn't mean erasing the love; it means allowing it to continue. It doesn't mean pretending it didn't change you or denying how deeply it moved you. It means you stop holding it so tightly that it starts to choke the life out of your present. You no longer need it to fit inside a label to prove that it matters. Because it did. It still does. But now it's time to let the *label* go so you can live your life.

These tools are not about rejection—they're about reverence. About closing a sacred chapter with honor so you can walk forward in truth.

Let this be a ceremony of release—not to forget what was, but to make room for what's becoming.

Journal Prompts: Unravel the Label

Before you begin, find a quiet space. Pour you a cup of tea if it helps you feel grounded. This is about honesty, not judgment. Let your pen do the talking:

- What have I made this label mean about my worth, my time-line, or my healing?
- If I could never define this connection again—how would I describe what it *felt* like?
- What part of me is afraid to let go of this identity? What is it trying to protect?
- What would I be free to experience if I stopped needing this to "mean" something?

Write freely. Let your hand guide you to the answers your heart has already whispered.

Write until your breath softens, your chest opens, and the need for certainty loosens its grip.

Ritual of Reverent Release: Burn the Label

This isn't a rejection. This is closure. This is you marking the moment you chose peace over proof.

On a small piece of paper, write down every label, title, or term you've used to define this connection—

Twin flame. Divine masculine. Karmic partner. Mirror soul. Runner. Chaser. Separation. Union. Whatever you've held tightly—write it down.

Pause. Hold the paper in your hands like you would a love letter. Place your palm over your heart and speak gently:

"I release the need to name what is sacred.
I release the pressure to make this anything other than what it
already was.
I honor the love. I thank the path.
And I return to my center now."

Burn the paper safely—outside, in a bowl, or over a candle flame. Let the smoke rise like a prayer. Let the ashes fall like closure. This is your declaration that you're no longer bound to the title—only to your truth.

Affirmation to Anchor the Soul's Truth

Repeat this to yourself in the mirror, write it on your bathroom wall, and whisper it when the ache creeps in. Let it become your new internal compass:

"I release the label. I trust the love.
I surrender to the mystery and open to what's next.
I am not lost—I am aligned.
I am not waiting—I am becoming."

Let these words sink in, not just as thoughts—but as a vibration. A lived truth. A signal to the Universe that you're ready. Not just for someone else to come in—but for your own next chapter to begin.

The Freedom to Let Love Be What It Is

There comes a moment on this path—after the rituals, after the signs, after the silence—when you stop asking, *"What is this?"* and start asking, *"What is this teaching me?"* For me, that moment wasn't loud or dramatic. It was quiet. It arrived on the heels of another surrender, another round of trying to hold it all together, another ache that reminded me the real reunion wasn't something I could force into form—it was something I had to find within.

The deeper I went, the more I realized that I had built my identity around a connection that cracked me open. I had called it sacred. I had named it a *twin-flame journey.* And in doing so, I gave it the power to shape my entire path. But eventually, the label that once felt like a lifeline began to feel like a leash. It boxed in my healing.

It distorted my worth. And it convinced me that love had to come through one person, one path, one story.

But the truth is that we only call them "twin flame" because of what they activated in us.

It's not about who they are. It's about who we become.

And yet, I understand why we cling to it. When your soul is waking up, and your heart is shattering, you *need* something to hold onto. You need a name for the fire. You need a map for the mystery. So yes—I still use the words. Not because I need them, but because you might. Because they're the keywords that brought you to this page. Because they're the breadcrumbs that lead us to the medicine we didn't know we were searching for.

But beyond the label? This isn't about them.

This is about you. It always was.

Because if the connection showed you anything, it was that love lives within you. That the deepest ache wasn't for someone else—it was for the part of yourself you abandoned long ago. And no title, no timeline, and no external reunion can fill the space that only self-commitment can reach.

We don't become whole by finding someone who fits our missing pieces. We become whole when we stop needing to be fixed. When we stop hustling for worthiness. When we stop healing just to prove we're ready. When we stop performing for the Universe and start living like we *are* the miracle.

So, let's drop the idea that we have to earn love by suffering.

Let's stop believing that we have to perfect ourselves to be seen. Let's stop mistaking pain for proof and absence for alignment. Let's stop trying to manifest love by chasing ghosts—and start anchoring love by choosing ourselves.

The point is this: if you want the ultimate love, you must first build it within yourself.

That's what I've done. I've stopped waiting for the story to finish in someone else's return. I've stopped asking for a sign to prove I'm worthy. I've stopped giving my power away to future possibilities. And I've started showing up like someone who already knows she is the miracle.

Maybe they were my twin flame. Perhaps they weren't. Maybe they'll return. Maybe they were never meant to stay. I no longer need certainty. Because the real miracle... was never them.

It was me.

The woman I became in their reflection. The woman who now creates her own peace builds her own home and chooses herself— over and over, without apology.

That is the reunion I was always meant to have.

So, I bless the story. I bless the connection. And I let it breathe— without needing it to define me, without needing it to last in form to last in meaning.

I used to think love would arrive once I had finally done enough. Healed enough. Aligned enough. What if I just cleared every block, passed every spiritual test, and held space through every silence? The Universe would reward me—with the one. With union. With the happy ending, I thought I'd earned it.

But what I didn't see then was that I wasn't healing to be worthy of love.

I was healing to remember I already was.

Some people do end up with the person they once called their twin flame. Others don't.

However, the point was never the person—it was always the process.

The journey doesn't lead you to them.
It leads you back to you.

And that's the truth I couldn't see until I stopped chasing the story and started living the lesson.

Because even the most divine connection is still a mirror. And whether they stay or disappear, reflect your light, or trigger your wounds, their role is not to complete you. It's to awaken you. To help you reclaim the parts of yourself that forgot their own power. To remember your wholeness. To come home to your own divinity.

So, yes, I still use the term' *twin flame*'—because it's how we find each other.

But the destination was never them.

It was always you.
You are your own flame.
You are the one you've been waiting for.

And when you finally claim that—fully, fiercely, without apology— nothing and no one can take it from you.

CHAPTER 12
FROM SPELLBOUND TO SOVEREIGN

The obsession didn't break me—it fueled the
flame I now embody.

You didn't make it up. The ache. The obsession. The all-consuming pull that hijacked your nervous system and whispered, *this is it.* The one. The mirror. The destined counterpart. It didn't come from nowhere—and it didn't mean you were broken. What you were experiencing wasn't weakness. It was an initiation. The moment the spell began, it didn't arrive with clarity. It came like wildfire—raw, sacred energy looking for a place to land. And because no one teaches us how to hold that kind of fire, we hand it to someone else. We project it onto a person, a label, a fantasy of rescue or reunion. We tell ourselves they're the key. They're the purpose. They're the source of the love we ache to feel. And just like that, the spell takes hold—not to punish us, but to crack us open.

This chapter is not about denying that spiral. It's about honoring what it taught you. Because obsession wasn't your downfall—it was your initiation. Every breakdown. Every late-night search for meaning. Every intuitive hit, unanswered text, spiritual sign, and whispered prayer was part of the sacred forge. Not to destroy you—but to burn away everything you weren't. And what remains now is something unshakable. You're not here to beg the Universe for a sign anymore. You've become the sign. You're no longer waiting to be chosen. You are the chooser.

Stepping into your power is the moment when everything integrates. When you stop romanticizing the chaos and start revering your sovereignty. You are not bound to the past. You are not waiting on a timeline. You are not spellbound by someone else's awakening. You are sovereign. And from this place, the rest of your life begins.

The Fire That Freed Me

I didn't just study this journey—I lived it, breathed it, burned in it. For over a decade, I danced with the twin-flame obsession, not as a distant observer but as someone knee-deep in the craziness, facedown in the storm. I moved through every phase, every false breakthrough that felt like freedom—until it cracked me open all over again. I bought into every belief. I decoded every dream. I clung to every 11:11 as if it were a divine contract sealed in stardust. Not because I didn't know better but because I needed to know it for myself. To teach it with integrity, I had to embody it. I had to spiral through it, burn through it, rise from it.

And I did. But the rising didn't come without loss. In fact, it took losing almost everything. For ten years, my relationships were portals. Each one mirrored my unmet needs, my abandoned self, and my addiction to the idea that one day—finally—love would arrive and save me. And just when I thought, "This must be the last layer," another one appeared. It felt like a spiritual Russian doll—each breakthrough concealing another becoming inside it.

Then came the voice—the soul truth that wouldn't let me stay asleep. It came in meditation first, but I felt it in every cell: *You have to let go of everything... to have everything.* And so the unraveling began. The final shattering wasn't a moment—it was a season. A wave that started before I left Sedona and kept crashing long after I did. I was already making moves to let go, to create space, to stop carrying what was no longer mine. But that truth, that soul whisper, gave me the strength to follow through. I sold everything. I condensed my life into two suitcases and one decision: to follow the flame that was no longer outside of me. I chose to become the one I had been waiting for.

That decision wasn't just spiritual—it was structural. It impacted everything. It meant surrendering the life I had built, the dynamics I had accepted, and the roles I no longer wanted to play. And as I stepped into that truth, the final unraveling began.

I had fully moved into my feminine role. And for the first time, I needed my partner at the time to step into his masculine role. I was stepping out of the role of being the man in the dynamic. I had led for too long and carried too much. And I had reached my edge. I shared my needs clearly. My lease was coming to an end, and I had no plans to renew it. I had built a life that no longer aligned with the version of me I was becoming. That little girl inside me needed a break from responsibilities. She needed rest. She needed to be held. And I needed him to show me I wasn't going to have to do it all alone.

So I asked him to take the lead—to figure out where we would live and how we would move forward. It wasn't about blaming him. It was about choosing me. It was about asking for partnership instead of continuing to push through on my own. When he didn't take action, I did. I began selling everything. I started making plans. My decision to move forward reflected the lack of movement I saw in him. And that mirrored something profound—a truth I couldn't ignore anymore. His reaction was immediate. Defensive. Triggered. He lashed out, not because of what I did but because my action highlighted what he hadn't done. And when the energy turned dark, and the blame began to build, I knew I couldn't sacrifice my peace to protect his wounds.

I asked him to leave by the end of the month. He did. But what followed was a storm I never saw coming. He filed charges against me—for not giving him a 30-day notice. The case went not just local, not just state, but federal. Because we had both left the state. It dragged on for nearly five months before it was finally dismissed.

In the meantime, I endured a smear campaign and watched him use my name to raise money while painting himself as the victim of my success. It hurt. But it didn't break me.

By then, I had already chosen the high road. I didn't retaliate. I didn't point fingers. I took responsibility for my part, for my energy, for my choices. I recognized how my inability to receive had been the very thing he was helping me heal. All the nurturing he provided became the gift I would eventually offer others. For the first time in my life, I understood what it meant to be nurtured. And I realized why I hadn't known how to nurture my children in the way they needed. Because I didn't know how to receive it myself.

My mother was one of the most nurturing individuals I have ever known. She loved me dearly. But I had pushed love away for years because I didn't know how to be vulnerable. I didn't know how to stay open in my feminine. That experience taught me. It humbled me. It healed me. And it empowered me.

I would never again look outside of myself for someone to fill something only I could fill from within. And while the cost was high—emotionally, financially, energetically—the return was infinite. These were lessons no amount of money could have bought. And walking through the fire didn't just burn away what was false. It revealed what was true.

That was the moment I stopped looking for someone to carry me. Because I remembered—I was never broken. I was becoming. Not in metaphor. In body. In blood. In breath. In choice. That wasn't the death of love. It was the resurrection of me. And from that moment forward, I vowed—no matter what came next—nothing would take me from myself again.

Obsession Is a Portal: The Shadow Path to Awakening

For years, I tried to escape it—the spiral, the ache, the all-consuming obsession that felt like it had imprinted my nervous system and rewired my reality. I wanted it gone. It felt like a curse. I tried to fix it, heal it, meditate it away. But what I've come to know deep in my bones is this: the obsession was never the problem. It was the portal.

Living the obsession wasn't a weakness; it was a passion. It wasn't madness. It wasn't because I loved too much or couldn't let go. It was because something inside me—something ancient, primal, sacred—was trying to break through. Obsession is sacred energy without a container. It's raw devotion with nowhere to land. It's the soul's fire rising before the mind knows what to do with it. And when that fire doesn't yet know where to burn, it reaches for the nearest thing that resembles home.

So, of course, it latched onto them. Of course, it circled around the one who lit it up. Not because they were the destination—but because they were the spark. The mirror. The illusion of completion that carried just enough truth to awaken everything I hadn't yet claimed in myself. That's why it felt so magnetic. That's why it was so hard to walk away. Because obsession wasn't about them—it was about what they reflected back to me.

They mirrored my capacity to love beyond reason. My willingness to feel without apology. My belief in something bigger than logic. My ache to give myself fully to something that stirred my soul. And none of that was wrong. It was just unanchored. It hadn't yet found its way home. So I did what most of us do when we don't yet know how to hold that level of energy—I gave it away. I poured my sacred fire into someone who couldn't contain it. Someone who didn't ask for it. Someone who couldn't return it.

Not because I was broken. But because I hadn't yet learned how to burn for myself.

That's what obsession really is. It's the seed of your purpose before it's planted. It's the electricity of your soul before it finds a circuit. It's power—untamed, unrefined, and waiting to be directed inward. The intensity you felt wasn't proof you were out of control. It was proof you were potent. You just hadn't been initiated into your own power yet.

But now? Now you see it. Now you know. The obsession didn't ruin you—it revealed who you are. It illuminated the parts of yourself still unclaimed. The child who wanted to be chosen. The healer who craved being needed. The lover who longed to be seen. And instead of shaming those parts, you can meet them now. With compassion. With reverence. With the knowing that your fire was never too much—it was just waiting for someone to hold it. And that someone… is you.

So no, you don't need to curse the spiral anymore. You don't need to regret the obsession or try to erase the way it moved through you. You can honor it as part of your becoming. As the shadow path to your awakening. Because now, you're not just someone who survived the spiral.

You are the one who turned it into a throne.

You Were Never Meant to Stay in the Fire—Only to Be Forged by It

There was a time when I thought the pain would never end. That the spiral, the obsession, the aching confusion was my new normal. I lived inside the fire—burning, breaking, begging for relief. But what I didn't know then is what I now hold as sacred truth: the fire was never meant to consume me. It was meant to change me.

This journey—this wild, sacred path of love and loss and longing—was not designed to keep you stuck in suffering. It was designed to initiate your rise. To strip away everything false so the truth of who you are can finally stand uncovered. You weren't sent into the flames to be punished. You were sent to be forged.

Every tear you cried rewired your nervous system for depth. Every sleepless night, you whispered prayers into the dark, stretching your soul into devotion. Every morning, you woke up still aching—but still breathing—strengthened a kind of resilience no one could take from you. Yes, the connection broke something open. But in that breaking, you found what was buried. Your boundaries. Your voice. Your power.

You learned to feel grief without numbing. To sit in silence without collapsing. To face rejection without translating it into worthlessness. You spoke your truth when it trembled. You walked away while your heart still ached. You became the woman—or man—who doesn't just survive the pain... but alchemizes it.

Make this your new truth: the spiral didn't break you. It built you. That connection you thought was here to complete you? It was here to confront you. To crack open every pattern of over-giving, over-chasing, and over-proving your worth. To expose the places where you didn't yet believe you deserved love without pain.

And now? You've stood in those flames. You've screamed. Collapsed. Raged. Begged. Lost. And yet—you are still here. The fire didn't take you. It transformed you. It scorched the parts of you that needed to die... so the truth of you could rise.

You don't need closure anymore. You don't need a text, a return, or a sign. Because you've become the sign. You've become the flame. You've become the living proof that healing is not a concept—it's a choice made in the middle of the burn.

This is your sacred fire. This is the moment you stop spiraling and start standing. So brush off the ash. Lift your head. Feel your spine lengthen. Let your breath anchor you in the now. You are not who you were when this began. You're no longer the seeker.

You are the sovereign.

And from here, you don't just walk forward—you rise.

You Were Being Initiated Into Power, Self, and Love

There was a time when I kept asking, *Why did it have to be this hard?* Why did it take that much pain to wake me up? I wanted answers, and I wanted them fast. But what I eventually realized was that the intensity of my spiral wasn't punishment. It was preparation. Every moment that broke me was also shaping me. The obsession, the longing, the overwhelming ache in my chest that made me question my sanity—all of it was sacred. Every trigger was an invitation. Every silence was a mirror. Every breakdown was burning away everything that wasn't truly me.

This connection wasn't just a heartbreak. It was an initiation. A deep soul-level activation calling me into power, self, and love—the kind of love that doesn't abandon itself just to be held by someone else. The connection showed me where love hadn't yet landed inside of me. It excavated my shadow, pulled my wounds to the surface, and revealed the places I still hadn't chosen myself.

I didn't know it at the time, but every spiral was sacred. Every day I rose again after sleepless nights was a quiet revolution. I wasn't broken. I was being rebuilt. The obsession wasn't a flaw. It was fire. I just hadn't learned how to hold that fire for myself yet. So I gave it to them. I poured my devotion into a connection that was meant to activate—not complete—me. I wasn't failing at love. I was shedding illusions. I didn't lose my twin flame. I found my truth. I stopped making someone else the portal to my purpose. I became the portal.

I learned to feel without collapsing. To speak without apologizing. To stay with myself when no one else did. I became the one who could sit in the fire, not begging to be rescued but discovering she could walk herself out. This wasn't the ending I had imagined. But it was the rebirth my soul had chosen. And now? I don't carry wounds. I carry wisdom. I don't chase love. I embody it. I don't just survive the spiral. I rise from it.

Now, the Path Is Yours to Walk

You made it—not because they came back, or the signs finally aligned, or some destiny played out precisely the way you wanted. You made it because you stopped giving your future away to someone else's timeline. You stopped tying your worth to their awakening. You realized that no external confirmation could match the internal clarity that had finally landed in your bones.

This is the place where the spiral ends. Not with perfect closure. Not with a reunion. But with a return—to your own soul. You no longer need an apology to heal. You no longer mistake their silence for your inadequacy. You no longer need one more card reading or late-night messages from the Universe to know what's true.

Because now, you trust yourself.

From here forward, you stop replaying what could've been. You stop living in the pause. You stop making your life small just in case they wake up. And instead? You wake up for you. You rebuild your life around truth, not trauma. You nourish the version of you who already feels chosen—because you finally chose yourself first.

You become the partner you were always waiting for.

This isn't about forgetting the connection. It's about releasing the contract that kept you bound to suffering. It's about taking everything the journey gave you and using it to create a future that reflects your worth—not your wounds. You're not discarding the love. You're expanding the outcome. You're not letting go of the truth. You're stepping fully into it.

Because love doesn't ask you to wait forever. Love asks you to *live.*

And you? You are the creator now. You hold the pen. You set the vision. You write the next chapter. Not from longing—but from embodiment. Not from lack—but from knowing.

There's nothing left to chase. Nothing left to prove. Nothing left to fix. What remains is you—glorious, grounded, and God-aligned. So take a breath. Take the step. This isn't the end of your story. It's the beginning of the one only you can write.

Stepping Into the Sacred Self: Integration Tools for Rebirth

You didn't just let go of a person. You let go of the version of yourself who believed you had to earn love to feel worthy. This was never about a single relationship—it was about the revolution that happened inside you. Now, everything you've been through becomes embodied wisdom. Integration isn't a concept—it's a recalibration. These tools are here to help you anchor the remembrance: you were never broken. You were being reborn.

The New Narrative: Writing the Truth of Who You've Become

When you put pen to paper, you give voice to the parts of you that once stayed silent. Let these journal prompts guide you into clarity—not just about what happened, but about what it revealed. Ask yourself: *How has this experience awakened parts of me I once abandoned? What do I now know about love, self-worth, and power that I didn't before? Who am I becoming—now that I'm no longer obsessed, waiting, or chasing? What sacred truths am I carrying forward into my next chapter?* Don't edit your truth. Let it pour. Let it roar. Let it reclaim you.

The Rise Ritual: A Ceremony of Return

This isn't just a practice. It's a rite of passage. Light a candle—not for them, but for the part of you that has made it through the fire. Stand barefoot, grounded in the now, and place one hand on your heart and the other on your womb, belly, or solar plexus. Close your eyes. Feel your breath. Feel your power. Then speak this aloud as a declaration:

> *"I am no longer who I was.*
> *I honor the fire that forged me.*
> *I release the past with reverence.*
> *I carry the wisdom, the love, and the power.*
> *I walk as love.*
> *I speak as truth.*
> *I move as freedom.*
> *I am whole.*
> *I am home."*

Pause. Let the words echo through your field. Let them sink into your bones. You are not the same. And you're not supposed to be.

The Frequency of Sovereignty: Your Daily Activation

Your words are spells, and this one is a mantra of remembrance. Say it. Sing it. Write it on your mirror until every cell knows the truth:

> *"I was not broken—I was being reborn.*
> *The obsession was the spell.*

But I am the sovereign.
I carry the fire now."

Repeat it every morning, every night, every time you feel the old story trying to creep back in. Because this time, you're not waiting to be chosen. You're not chasing the flame. You are it.

You Were Initiated by Obsession—Now You Rise in Embodiment

You've made it. Not because someone came back to love you but because you finally came back to yourself. After all the spirals, all the signs, all the sleepless nights wondering if you were losing your mind—or your soul—you stand here, not as the one who chased, but as the one who chose. Chose to stay. Chose to rise. Decided to rewrite the story, not with desperation, but with devotion to something deeper than any label could hold: your sacred self.

This wasn't just a heartbreak. This was a holy reckoning. A dismantling of every illusion you once believed about what it meant to be worthy of love. You were initiated through obsession, yes—but you didn't stay there. You didn't bow to the ache or collapse under the waiting. You let the ache become your altar. You let the waiting sharpen your wisdom. You let the fire cleanse everything that wasn't real. And in doing so, you reclaimed your light—not as a beacon begging to be found, but as a flame that never needed to be rescued in the first place.

Now, you no longer perform for love. You no longer plead for someone else to see your value. You walk in it. You speak from it. You build from it. You live as it is. This isn't the moment you wait for another sign. This is the moment you become one. Because what you've just walked through wasn't meant to end in reunion—it was meant to end in resurrection.

You are no longer the seeker. You are the signal. You are no longer writing someone else into the center of your story. You are the center. You are not here to prove your worth to someone who couldn't hold it. You are here to embody it so fully the world has no choice but to meet you in your truth or move out of your way.

So take this fire and use it. Not to burn down what was but to ignite what's next. Let your voice shake the air. Let your love build legacies. Let your radiance take up space. You are not a chapter in someone else's return. You are the return. To self. To power. To presence. To peace.

This isn't where the story ends. It's where it finally becomes yours.

Now go.

Live like the one who made it through the madness. Speak like the one who remembered their magic. Walk like the one who never needed to be chosen—because you chose yourself.

You were forged in obsession. But you rise in embodiment.

And from here?

You're just getting started.

CONCLUSION
BECOMING THE FLAME

*They didn't awaken me. The fire did. And now—I
am the flame.*

You are not the same person who picked up this book. That version of you—the one who was spiraling in signs, drowning in longing, and searching the internet at 2 a.m. for answers to explain why your heart wouldn't stop aching—has died a thousand deaths throughout these pages. And each one brought you closer to something more true. More grounded. More real. More you.

Because this book wasn't just a guide. It was a mirror, a match, a funeral, and a flame. It asked you to let go of the illusion. To confront the ache. To face the version of you who believed love had to come through someone else to be real.

You didn't just walk through the fire—you let it burn what no longer belonged. And somewhere between the obsession, the collapse, and the ache that felt like it might undo you, you found something holy in the ashes. You found yourself.

You faced your own reflection in the shattered mirror and didn't look away. You grieved, you unraveled, you released. And still, you rose. Not the same. Not broken. But reborn.

Because this wasn't a journey meant to be survived. It was meant to be alchemized. You didn't just make it through the fire. You became it.

What You Thought Was Love—Was Really the Flame Calling You Home

For so long, it felt like love. The ache. The pull. The highs and lows wrapped themselves around your nervous system, making it hard to breathe without thinking of them. It felt fated. Cosmic. Sacred. Like they were the missing piece to everything, you didn't know how to give yourself. But now you know the truth: it wasn't just about them. It was never really about them. It was about your soul's desire to return to wholeness—masked as romantic obsession.

The person you were chasing was never the destination. They were the spark. The catalyst. The sacred disruptor that cracked open everything in you that wasn't in alignment. You weren't just trying to win back a connection—you were trying to fill the void where your own love, safety, and sovereignty had gone missing.

What you thought was love was actually the fire calling you home.

Because real love doesn't demand that you lose yourself. It doesn't ask you to abandon your needs, question your worth, or settle for breadcrumbs laced with "divine timing." The twin flame didn't complete you—they revealed who you are. They mirrored back the parts of you still waiting to be chosen, still aching to be seen. And in the end, it was never about being reunited with them. It was about being reunited with yourself.

This wasn't a punishment. It was a portal. A sacred wake-up call disguised as heartbreak. And you were never meant to stay asleep.

The Mirror Shattered So You Could See Yourself Clearly

When the mirror cracked, it hurt like hell. Because for a long time, you thought it was the reflection that made you whole. You believed that their presence was proof of your worth, that their recognition was the answer to your ache. But when everything shattered— when the silence stretched too long, the signs lost their meaning, and the fantasy could no longer hold its shape—you were left with the one thing that had been waiting all along: the truth.

The twin flame wasn't here to give you your identity. They were here to remind you of what you had forgotten. That you were never incomplete. That your love didn't need a name to be real. That you didn't need to suffer to prove your devotion. And as painful as it was to watch the dream dissolve, it was in that very dissolution that something sacred emerged. You.

You didn't lose your other half. You found your whole self.

That mirror shattered not to destroy you but to reveal you. Every cracked piece held a version of you that had been abandoned in the pursuit of being chosen. And now, standing in the aftermath, you can finally see the whole picture—not the fantasy, not the role, not the projection—but the raw, radiant truth of who you really are. Not broken. Not chasing. Not waiting. Just real. Just whole. Just home.

You Are No Longer the Chaser—You Are the Flame

You don't chase anymore. Not because you stopped caring but because you started remembering who you are. The one who once begged for signs, waited for replies, and tried to decode energy that couldn't even meet you with words—is gone. That version of you was birthed in survival, shaped by longing, fueled by the ache of abandonment. But now? You've risen from the ruins of that story. You no longer seek validation in someone else's recognition. You no longer need to be claimed. Because you've claimed yourself.

You are the flame now.

You stopped waiting for someone to choose you and started choosing yourself. You stopped contorting to be understood and began expanding into your full expression. You no longer need closure because you've become the closure. The love you once thought had to come through them? It lives in you now—steady, grounded, undeniable.

This isn't about giving up on love. It's about finally knowing the difference between chasing a fantasy and becoming a match for something real. You no longer need the signs to tell you what you already feel. You no longer need the label to justify the connection. You don't need to prove the sacredness of what happened. You lived it. You learned from it. And now you lead yourself forward.

The chaser energy has dissolved. The seeking has burned. And all that remains is a steady fire that radiates from within you—not desperate, not waiting, not needing to be seen—but illuminating everything around you because it finally sees *you*.

Your New Love Story Starts With You

The love story you thought you were writing was never about someone else. It was always leading you back here—to this moment, where the only reunion that truly matters is the one happening inside of you. After all the unraveling, all the longing, all the reaching for someone to meet you in the fire… you became the one, not in theory, but in truth. And now, you don't need anyone to rescue you from the ashes. You *are* the resurrection.

This is where the real story begins. Not with being chosen but with choosing yourself. Not with fantasy but with embodiment. Not with waiting, but with walking forward, steady and whole, knowing that love is no longer something you beg for—it's something you *are*. And from this place, what's meant for you can't help but find you. Not because you forced it. Not because you performed for it. But because you finally stopped chasing what was never capable of meeting you, and started becoming someone who meets themselves fully.

This isn't the end of your love story. This is the part where you stop settling for potential and start allowing love that's rooted in truth to rise. Love that doesn't require shrinking, performing, or waiting in pain. Reciprocal love. Expansive. Safe. Sacred. Whether that comes from a partner, your community, or the quiet power you now hold in your own presence—it starts with you.

So no, you didn't lose love. You just stopped looking for it where it was never meant to be. And in doing so, you made space for what's real.

Integration and Initiation — When the Old Pulls You Back

Just because the obsession has lifted doesn't mean the ache won't try to return. Healing doesn't unfold in straight lines. It moves in spirals—loops of remembering and forgetting, softening and strengthening. There will be moments when something triggers the past. When the pull creeps back in, when your chest tightens, when your mind whispers, *"Maybe it really was meant to be."* That's not failure. That's an invitation.

In those moments, don't spiral. Breathe. Ground. Return. You've walked this path before, but now you meet it differently. With more awareness. With deeper roots. With a fire inside you that won't let you abandon yourself again for a feeling wrapped in fantasy. The difference now is that you no longer mistake the ache for love—you recognize it as a memory calling you to stay awake.

Let it come. Let it move through you. But don't give it your power. You've already claimed that. And every time you choose yourself again, you reinforce the new story. The one where you don't chase love. You *are* love. Where you don't need closure. You *embody* it. Where you don't wait for someone to see you. You are already fully seen—by the version of you who refused to settle for pain disguised as destiny.

This is the integration. The holy remembering. The initiation that says:

You're ready now. Not just to let go—but to live free.

WHAT'S NEXT? KEEP RISING

This book may be closing, but your journey is far from over.
You've broken the spell.
You've reclaimed your power.
You've become the flame.

Now it's time to rise!

Whether you're still integrating or ready to step fully into your next chapter, I've created ongoing support to help you embody your transformation and live it out—day by day, choice by choice, flame by flame.

1. Explore More Ways to Work With Me

From transformational retreats and breakthrough sessions to future books, advanced mentoring, and spiritual business guidance, you'll find a range of ways to connect, grow, and receive personalized support.
Explore offerings at: www.TwinFlameExpert.com

Scan the QR code below to visit directly:

2. Deepen Your Healing with Courses and Tools

Inside **Ascension Academy Online**, you'll find a private library of self-paced courses, meditations, and energetic tools designed to support nervous system regulation, soul reinvention, and spiritual empowerment.
Begin your next chapter at: www.AscensionAcademyOnline.com

Scan the QR code below to explore courses:

3. Watch Free Videos and Energy Updates

Subscribe on YouTube for free guidance, energy updates, meditations, and tools to support your transformation and twin flame journey.

Find me at: **YouTube.com/**@TwinFlameExpert

Scan the QR code below to subscribe instantly:

Thank you for walking through the fire with me.
The next chapter is yours to live.

And it's only getting brighter from here.

About Dr. Harmony

Dr. Harmony is a best-selling author, transformational mentor, and renowned twin-flame expert known for her grounded wisdom and soul-shifting guidance. With over two decades of experience in energy healing, spiritual psychology, and vibrational medicine, she has helped thousands worldwide break free from toxic patterns, awaken their power, and step into sovereignty.

As a pioneer in the twin-flame space, *Dr. Harmony* is celebrated for her no-fluff, soul-deep approach to healing. Her signature blend of science, spirit, and self-empowerment has guided seekers through the darkest nights of obsession and into the light of embodiment.

In her raw and transformational work, she helps you break the spell of obsession, reclaim your energy, and uncover the truth beneath the fantasy. Her teachings go beyond labels and timelines, calling you back to the only reunion that was ever guaranteed: *the one with yourself.*

Whether through her books, courses, or retreats, *Dr. Harmony* creates sacred spaces for radical healing, nervous system repair, and profound spiritual transformation. She invites you not just to let go, but to rise.

Connect with Dr. Harmony:

Visit www.TwinFlameExpert.com for resources, retreats, and upcoming books.

Explore online programs at www.AscensionAcademyOnline.com.

Follow on social media **@TwinFlameExpert** for inspiration, insights, and live updates.

www.ingramcontent.com/pod-product-compliance
Lightning Source LLC
Chambersburg PA
CBHW071428090426
42737CB00011B/1598